ISBN-13: 978-0985002749 (WIN Publishing)
ISBN-10: 0985002743

FIRST EDITION

This publication is designed to provide accurate and authoritative information in regard to the subject matter covered. It is sold with the understanding that neither the author nor the publisher is engaged in rendering legal, accounting, or other professional service. If legal advice or other expert assistance is required, the services of a competent professional person should be sought.

- From a Declaration of Principles jointly adopted by a Committee of the American Bar Association and a Committee of Publishers.

WIN Publishing books are available at quantity discounts to use as premiums and sales promotions, or for use in corporate training programs. For more information, please email jwilhoit@win-rei.com.

Wilhoit Investment Network, LLC performs acquisitions and asset management of quality multifamily developments. Our focus is on commercial grade apartment properties. We work with owners of both public and private sector assets to create value based on proactive asset management and the implementation of strategies to enhance financial and operational efficiencies.

John Wilhoit is the author of three books: How To Read A Rent Roll: A Guide to Understanding Rental Income and Multifamily Insight Vol 1 and Vol 2 How to Acquire Wealth Through Buying the Right Multifamily Assets in the Right Markets.

Join our PowerHour Leadership Academy focused on
G.R.A.C.E [Growing Revenue & Controlling Expenses].
http://www.powerhourleadershipacademy.com/pm/

For 50+ hours of property management audio training,
4 books and live weekly leadership academy–surf here,
http://www.multifamilyinsight.net/book

**Websites**

http://www.multifamilyinsight.net (blog)

http://www.multifamilyinsight.com (website)

http://www.rentrolltriangle.com

http://www.win-rei.com (Company)

http://www.linkedin.com/in/johnwilhoit

http://www.twitter.com/johnwilhoitjr

## About the Multifamily Insight Blog:

Mr. Wilhoit's blog, Multifamily Insight, is dedicated to assisting current and future multifamily property owners, operators and investors in executing specific tasks that allow multifamily assets to operate at their highest level of efficiency. He writes about real world issues in multifamily property management and acquisitions. http://www.MultifamilyInsight.net

# About the Author:

John Wilhoit is President of Wilhoit Investment Network, LLC (WIN LLC). His career has focused on large-scale multifamily communities including market rate and mixed-finance developments. Mr. Wilhoit has held positions with HUD, AIMCO and the Maryland Housing fund. John's formal education includes a Bachelor's of Science degree in Business Management with a minor in Economics from Pepperdine University and a Masters in Urban & Regional Planning with a focus on Urban Studies from Alabama A&M University.

WIN LLC provides consulting, asset management and market analysis services for multifamily property owners.

**WIN LLC**
**3610 Buttonwood Drive Suite 200**
**Columbia, MO 65201**

# Other Books by the Author

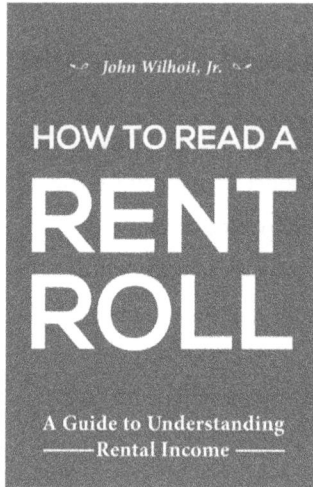

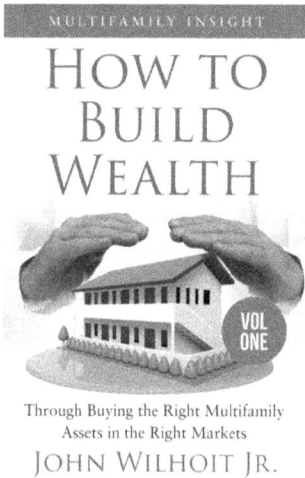

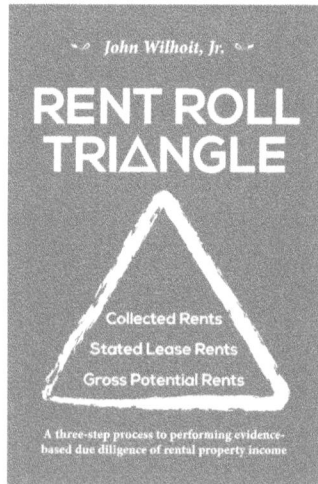

John Wilhoit, Jr.

## HOW TO READ A RENT ROLL

A Guide to Understanding
—— Rental Income ——

MULTIFAMILY INSIGHT

## HOW TO BUILD WEALTH

VOL ONE

Through Buying the Right Multifamily
Assets in the Right Markets

JOHN WILHOIT JR.

John Wilhoit, Jr.

## RENT ROLL TRIANGLE

Collected Rents

Stated Lease Rents

Gross Potential Rents

A three-step process to performing evidence-
based due diligence of rental property income

# Acknowledgments

Thanks to my many mentors that have broadened my horizons both professionally and personally. They are; Mr. John S. Wilhoit, Mrs. Alice Allen, Sr., Mr. George Eaton, Mr. Richard Mendenhall Mr. John Brown, Mr. Jerry O. Wilhoit and Mrs. Ella Wilhoit, Mr. Ernest Oriente of PowerHour and Mr. Kerry W. Kirby, Founder of *365 Connect* and *MultifamilyBiz.com.* Thanks also to my wife Dr. Della Streaty-Wilhoit for a lifetime of love and support.

# Multifamilyinsight <sub>.net</sub>

This blog is dedicated to assisting current and future multifamily property owners, operators and investors in executing specific tasks that allow multifamily assets to operate at their highest level of efficiency.

We discuss best practices in multifamily property management and methods related to how to buy multifamily apartment complexes. Our focus is on sharing strategies and tactics that can be implemented and measured.

We discuss real world issues in multifamily property management and acquisitions. This blog is intended to be informational only and does not provide legal, financial or accounting advice. Seek professional counsel.

Other Books by John Wilhoit:

**Multifamily Insight Vol 1:** How to Build Wealth Through Buying the Right Multifamily Assets in the Right Markets

**How to Read a Rent Roll:** A Guide to Understanding Rental Income

# Table of Contents

**Chapter 3**

## Chapter 4

## Chapter 5

# Introduction

Multifamily Insight Volume 2 is a continuation of the themes presented in Volume 1 related to multifamily acquisitions, property management, demographics & market analysis and finance. Each chapter provides a multitude of "knowledge bites" on Multifamily operations for your contemplation and consideration. There are ideas, action steps, and often, a recommended path to producing superior results.

The objective of this writing is to have a compilation of knowledge on multifamily acquisitions and property management in one place at one time, as a learning and reference guide for real world education and explanation of how to acquire and management commercial multifamily assets.

This book is a collection of the most popular editorial writing as presented on Multifamily Insight's blog. These articles focus on multifamily acquisitions, property management, market analysis and real estate finance. The fifth chapter is Opinion & Editorial with the focus being multifamily and the American economy. Guest Authors are denoted by their name proceeding the title.

We attempt to present here "ever-green" vignettes that will serve the reader for many years into the future. Like Adam Smith's Invisible Hand, many of the principles have a long history of being true. More specifically, I hope the thoughts presented will serve as a touchstone to expand your knowledge in the profession of multifamily acquisitions and property management.

Thank you for purchasing this book. It is the culmination of writing over a three-year span. Even still, the writing is not the hard part; it is the sitting to write that was most difficult.

# Chapter 1

## Multifamily
## Acquisitions

# Real Estate Investing with a Sense of Purpose

What do real estate equity and jet fuel have in common? Both can evaporate before your very eyes! Equity is the rocket fuel of real estate investing. Simplified the real estate cycle is equilibrium, growth, over–building (bubble), bust, recovery.

A rocket scientist never uses rocket fuel just for fun. Even in experimentation fuel usage is purposeful. The same is true for equity use in a real estate transaction. The energy and resources required to start and finish a commercial real estate transaction are significant. It is a serious endeavor with large financial ramifications.

The primary "sense of purpose" in any real estate investment should be, first, preservation of capital. Second is providing a return on investment (or targeted return) given the yield profile of investors.

Like any endeavor that includes the word "rocket" there are multiple systems required for a successful launch. Long before we see a rocket take to the sky years of work went into getting to the launch date. In the case of real estate investing, launch day is the day of closing. Getting to launch day takes months of preparation.

Excluding reliance on layered secondary financing (owner financing, mezzanine debt, debentures, cross–collateralization), equity represents the real dollars that are "at risk".

"All in" equity is the number that requires yield or a return on invested capital. The only sure way to determine yield is by accurately determining your costs basis.

Just like rocket launching, commercial real estate investing is no place for guess work or on–the–job learning. From the very first day resources are at risk to acquire real estate assets. Deploy these resources as efficiently as possible. If equity is the rocket fuel of real estate investing, prudent use with a high level of expertise is paramount. Always.

# Finding the Perfect Purchase

In real estate investing, finding the perfect multifamily asset to purchase has little to do with the actual real estate. Blink blink. What? No, really. Why? This is because any particular piece of real estate is only as important (read; as valuable) as the substance of its surroundings. Finding the perfect asset begins with quality market research.

Meaning: a specific real property asset is defined by the market dynamics represented in surrounding economic activity.

Saying a particular piece of property is perfect is like saying you have seen the perfect fastball. Even if this were true, how do you repeat it, again and again? By identifying markets with similar attributes to those surrounding your original premise (or perfect asset) then adjusting and making incremental improvement to the model.

For income property purchases other than trophy properties the market and submarket defines the asset. It is never the other way around.

The primary service providers of multifamily market data are similar to the well–known rating agencies of S&P and Moody's in that they tend to swing in the same direction in the broader scope of trends.

REIS, MP/F and Axiometrics are all quality service providers. Their forecast will vary on market specifics (sometimes significantly) but they all get it right on matters of national scope.

- **REIS**
- **MP/F**
- **Axiometrics**

Finding the perfect asset begins with quality market research. The three service providers noted above represent a good place to start.

# Multifamily Acquisitions and $4 Gasoline

The price of gasoline impacts every part of our lives from food production and delivery to the cars we drive and our selection of a place to live. Include real estate investing in this grouping.

In my self–imposed naiveté I believe oil prices should be $35–75 per barrel. What keeps prices above these levels are things unrelated to actual oil production; like presumed civil unrest, the 24–hour news cycle, three guys in Luxembourg hoarding contracts in an attempt to keep pressure on supply (when supply is excessive).

I remember Christmas 2008. This is a few short months after Lehman failed and the Troubled Asset Recovery Program (TARP– how many acronyms does it take to spend a billion dollars?) was all the rage in Washington, DC.

Momentarily, the national average for a gallon of gasoline was $1.72 a gallon. It was an economic "dark hour' and oil was $40 a barrel.

**When fixed costs rise, people "circle the wagons"**

Food, fuel and shelter are three unavoidable costs related to the "carbon footprint" of our existence. Increases in food, fuel or shelter means having to cut back in some other area. The most volatile of these expenditures is fuel. When fuel rises, renters look for ways to decrease their housing expenditures.

Here is the trade off: Rent a newer/bigger place for less money further away from your job and pay the difference in fuel consumption, or live closer to your job in a smaller place for more money, and pay less for fuel consumption. What most residents fail to realize is that rent growth is more likely at the close–in location.

Multifamily owners in tertiary markets become imperiled when fuel prices sky rocket as individuals and families who were previously willing to live the rural life and take on the commute can no longer justify this lifestyle as fuel prices increase.

Properties closer to job centers thrive, properties farther from job centers suffer. And, since oil prices are somewhat "sticky" on the way down, once this trend begins it reverses ever so slowly.

From a European perspective we Americans are wimps when it comes to our tolerance for pain at the pump. Consider fuel today in London and Paris is approaching $10 U.S. per gallon. Consider also that both of these cities have tremendous infrastructure in mass transit.

For "people transport" in many major U.S. cities we continue to utilize older "technology" called roads, rather than a spoke and hub tram system.

When reviewing potential acquisition candidates always consider proximity to jobs and rapid transit. Also check on the municipalities budget to maintain existing rapid transit systems. You don't want to be the last one to know that bus service that is now in front of your development is soon to be re–routed with the next closest stop a mile away.

In 2015, with fuel prices hovering around three dollars it seems like the pressure is off. The cyclical nature of commodity prices will continue.

# Top Ten Reasons to Own Multifamily

Why own apartments? While real estate investing is a contact sport with numerous pitfalls the rewards can be enormous. Positive outcomes require patience, expertise, access to capital and time with equal emphasis on all of these. Following are ten reasons to own multifamily.

**Immediate income**. With use of reasonable leverage (debt levels); immediate cash flow to investors is the draw to being in this sector. Over–leverage decreases cash flow, sometimes to the point of bringing it to zero. Price, leverage, occupancy and rent growth are the big determinants of immediate income.

**Eventual (significant) passive income**. While no investment is really passive, over time as cash flow increases there is more cash. Thus, capital expenditures reserves are fully funded with Net Operating Income (NOI) now reflecting true unobstructed free cash flow.

**Pending limited supply**. The construction pipeline in Multifamily practically came to a halt in 2008. Re–booting that pipeline has a very long glide path measured in years– not months. As population continues to tick upward, any significant move in GDP, or in-migration, will place extended pressure on supply. As of 2015, supply continues to lag demand.

**Capturing rent growth**. As more people become long–time renters, and as a result of less multifamily supply, the apartment industry should begin to see acceleration in rent growth. Some 24–hour cities are seeing near double–digit rent growth now.

**Appreciation**. Too many people believe appreciation is a function of inflation. While inflation is a component of appreciation the greatest factor increasing value is growth in NOI. Grow net operating income and see appreciation in value (no inflation required).

**Depreciation**. Tax benefits should be an ancillary reason for investing in the asset class. Yes, depreciation offsets current income, but it comes back around at time of sale (1031 notwithstanding).

**Trade Value**. While real estate requires time to trade, within the real estate asset classes multifamily has a very high level of interest and a deep buyer pool. When it's time to sell, multifamily has trade value with market times ranging from 6–12 months. That's a short porch in the commercial real estate world.

**Investment diversification**. Allocation theory suggests that a portfolio should have between 5% and 15% of assets in real estate (excluding your personal residence). Thus, investors should have $50,000 to $150,000 in real estate for every one million dollars in net worth. Granted, multifamily is only one type of "real estate", but given its trade value and other attributes this asset class has merit.

**Safety of capital.** Real estate prices dip, go sideways and rise over time, but less so with multifamily. Preservation of capital is a cornerstone of sound investment decisions and multifamily is a solid place for long–term investing.

**Inflation protector**. Predicting inflation is like betting on who will win the World Series before the season starts– there are just too many factors to consider. But when inflation does kick in, history shows that multifamily keeps pace.

# The Dangerous Game of No Money Down Deals

Attempting the old standard, "by the book," cookie cutter tactics lamely taught over and over again for single–family investing and applying them to commercial multifamily is a recipe for disaster. In fact, it is a very dangerous game as the end result is that you, the brand–spanking–new owner of that apartment property, probably have jeopardized your entire net worth for the privilege. Congratulations, cliff dweller.

When was the last time you were, figuratively speaking, thrown under a bus? With respect to nothing–down deals, too often people go willingly under the bus. Year in and year out we get emails seeking guidance on multifamily deals where the buyer has limited or no capital; the proverbial nothing down deal. Let me be succinct: DON'T DO IT! There. I said it.

Few people seem to appreciate this response prior to gushing with deal–specific particulars. Doesn't matter don't do it. I don't care if your uncle is giving you the deal of a lifetime. Sounds harsh, doesn't it? Let me explain.

Maybe your uncle is a really nice guy, you took care of him when he broke his ankle and he's doing a good deed in return. With a three million dollar deal where the first mortgage is two million and Good Uncle is taking back a second for a million, you are toast (good intentions or not).

First of all, on the surface, Good Uncle has set the purchase price at three million. Are you going to spend a few thousand on a commercial appraisal to validate that a reasonable price is three million? At this level of leverage (100% financing) every available dollar will be going to debt service. In reality, there will likely be a monthly deficit. How will your relations be if the payment due on the second mortgage is $5,000 monthly, but the asset is only kicking out $3,000 monthly? Uncle wants his money. After all, you bought the deal.

Second, what makes you so special? Why are you being offered this deal? Is it your good looks, because you dress well? What do you bring to the deal? Consider the following:

If the answer is the ability to "fog a mirror" and "sign a paper," then these talents have nothing whatsoever to do with acquiring a quality multifamily asset AND having skills to run the deal no matter the capital stack. **The capital stack** is just one component of Multifamily ownership and asset management. Yet so many people get caught up in this segment of the deal that every other aspect becomes diminished. This is tragic. Why? Because while getting this right is imperative, it is just one leg of the table. And a single strong leg does not a table make.

Most people selling a nothing–down deal are looking to get out of **Property Management**. Perhaps they didn't really know what they were getting into when they bought this asset and it's kicking their butt– property management, vendors, dealing with residents– this is not what they signed up for. After trying to sell the deal and failing, they come up with the bright idea to sell the deal to someone they know for nothing down. This is in the same category as living with you mother–in–law; it works sometimes, but is generally a bad idea.

So here you come, with limited input on **Deal Structure,** maybe some property management experience, and limited to **No Working Capital**. You are... crispy toast just waiting to happen.

It really boils down to **Capacity**. Yet, capacity by itself is not enough to make the deal work if every other aspect is out of whack with reality (including valuation).

So for those unconvinced, for the brave few who wish to proceed, please consider the following:

1. The transaction should be provided the same or more due diligence than any other deal–more actually because of the significant threat posed to your personal net worth.

2. The transaction should be arms length. Meaning even if the sellers are known to you, there are no short cuts. Hire the same service providers you would for any other deal; appraisal, closing, attorneys, environmental, etc.

3. Listen to your attorney with respect to the assumption of existing debt. Assuming a commercial loan has more thorns than any rose bush, getting it right requires quality counsel.

4. If Debt Service Coverage (DSC) is 1.0 or less ($1 of Net Operating Income to pay for $1 of monthly debt obligations) then you must have cash on hand to address any shortfall from day one. And for the next month, and the next if necessary. Otherwise you are dead in the water on the day of closing unless you have a source of funds for that unexpected, unanticipated, yet immediate, $5,000 monthly negative.

5. Identify and estimate the price for property management. If you have no experience in property management, this is not the time or place to learn the trade. If you do have property management experience, great, cost out work and time required to address the asset. If the time required to manage is beyond your abilities, then you must hire a manager or PM company. Factor these costs in.

Miss any of these steps and you, the original toast, will be as burnt as a pizza left in the oven overnight at 400 degrees. Note, this is just the starter list. Seek professional counsel every step of the way.

# Selling Multifamily: Five Hard Exit Strategies

In today's environment, exiting from an owned multifamily asset can be a tough nut to crack. Why? It would be easy to say "It's the times we live in." Well, yes, but that is not actionable. Selling multifamily today is difficult, primarily because people fail to recognize the time and complexity of the process. Buyers are there, assets are available...but the timeline is the thing.

Even the easy one's require serious expertise and a serious time commitment. Selling is as common as buying, of course, just recognize the timeline. Market time to a sale in primary markets is six to twelve months, longer in secondary and tertiary markets. Following are five reasons why it can be hard to sell a multifamily asset.

**Limited 1031 Exchange Activity**. Gone are the days you can wait on a hungry 1031 buyer that must invest NOW, NOW, NOW! They are few and far apart. When volume slows so does 1031 money. There are traders, but at what price glory? The only difference between a 1031 buyer and anyone else is that they have a definitive timeline to meet. Otherwise, they are the same as any other buyer.

Brokers are still the center of attention in buyer identification, but they have competition for product; LinkedIN®, Loopnet and a myriad of other on–line resources will provide multifamily assets with exposure. For those with limited experience in the asset class a broker is still your best bet. There are just too many landmines to guess on matters related to selling a commercial multifamily asset.

**Cash Buyers**. Cash buyers, fine. But cash at a punishing discount, is this viable? The offer is from a cash buyer with proof of funds letter in hand; so what. If the price and terms offered is out of bounds for you the seller, then pass. If the offer is within your strike zone, proceed.

People devote way too much time pondering buyer motivations. Assuming your bases are covered, meaning no environmental or structural issues are undisclosed, close the deal. Talk about buyer motivations at dinner with your investors while handing out checks.

**CMBS lock–outs**. The quantity of Commercial Mortgage Backed Securities (CMBS) loans with extended lock-out periods is huge. These lock–out periods were installed to protect mortgage investors by preserving yield for an extended period. That makes sense. And, borrowers/owners signed up willingly. Now comes the pain as deal after deal has egregious defeasance that drops a property into years of purgatory, of unsellable stasis.

Make certain to "know your loan." Can you sell now? Is there an added cost associated with liquidating this asset? What is this cost? Is the loan on your asset beyond the lock–out period? Who is your contact person for obtaining a payoff? Are they picking up the phone and responsive or lost in foreclosure/robo–document land?

**Loan Underwriting**. The stack of paper is thicker than ever at loan closings. And there are more attorneys than iPhones at the table. There is no way out. If you want the sale, facilitate the purchase by providing the required documentation... As a seller, this means being amiable to assisting the buyer in processing their loan package with lender-required documentation and updates all along the way.

**Time, Patience and Exposure**. These are your best friends in the selling process. All are equally important. Patience is the most difficult of all. Having all three of these in combination will assist any seller in navigating the items above. There is no replacement for time in a transaction. Each step has its own cadence.

# Multifamily's Best Kept Secret

Multifamily's best kept secret is no secret at all: long–term ownership provides significant financial rewards. Why do I call this a secret? Because so few take advantage of the power of income compounding that is included in the rewards of long–term ownership.

In its' simplest version, even if expenses keep pace with rents (rents rise 3%, expenses rise 3% year after year) then still, over time, debt is reduced. After a period of years (say five or more) when debt is refinanced at its' current balance (meaning no cash out at re–fi) then cash flow increases. Cash flow increases. Did I mention that cash flow increases?

**Buy and Hold...**

The wealthiest real estate investors I know are those who still own the same assets they purchased in the 1970's and 1980's. The SAME ASSETS. No bootstrapping into the latest and greatest over–leveraged deal, no trading up and up and up again. More often than not, the assets purchased "back in the day" are by far their smallest deals...but they still own them along with the larger portfolio, perhaps as a reminder of where they started-but probably because they are cash flowing like crazy.

You've heard of sellers remorse. I can think of story after story of people telling me about the asset they wished they'd never sold. How it's now worth ten times what they paid. Do we learn from our mistakes? Yes. The best of all worlds is that this learning allows us to avoid future mistakes. Buying apartments is hard work. Selling means having to find another similar and hopefully better asset given capital availability.

**The Ten Percent Rule**

One significant mistake that multifamily sellers make is taking cash from a sale and over–leveraging into the next deal. The types and kinds of justification are unending. The result is that everything has to go perfect for the newly purchased, over–leveraged deal to breakeven, much less cash flow. So the new owner, the one who sold a cash–flowing asset to purchase an over–leveraged asset now has eliminated the prior cash flow (that they were very accustom to seeing) in exchange for losing sleep over the new deal that, again, has to work perfect to breakeven.

A better idea is to move up, but in increments. Consider my 10% rule here; if the asset sold was leveraged at 50% then leverage the newly purchased asset by 60%. Applying this rule up to 80% loan–to–value will allow the newly purchased asset to have similar financing in place to the one sold, and similar cash flow. You, the seller and new buyer, gain a new depreciation schedule and peace of mind. That's a good combination!

**There is a time to sell...**

The important part to selling is to put in the "thinking time" prior to making the assets public. What's the end game? Where will funds be delivered one day after closing? Even seasoned pro's get the urge to sell. And here's the bad part; some people sell out of sheer boredom. I fear this happens all too often.

One investor I know sold his assets and purchased mutual funds. His reasoning was family members were in no position to "manage the managers" and with his purchase of mutual funds he was buying long–term, professional management requiring no active management by family members.

Certainly, there are a multitude of good reasons to sell a multifamily asset; from capturing capital gains for reinvestment, estate planning, repositioning corporate or personal assets, re–balancing a portfolio, use of proceeds to pursue other investments, tax planning.

Similar to interest income, re–investing in your multifamily assets pays dividends upon dividends. This is why avoiding capital expenditures is a bad idea...you are reducing the future value of the income stream by letting a property deteriorate. Before letting this occur you are better off selling the asset.

Avoiding the sale of an asset strictly based on tax considerations is short–sighted. Tax considerations are just one part of being in business. Warren Buffet is famous for saying he will be pleased to take on an investment others pass up because of fear of the big tax bill that comes with success.

Long–term ownership can be very very profitable. This is why the selection of the right markets and the right assets is so very important. When purchased and opperated professionally these same assets may be in your family's portfolio for generations.

# Quality, Speed or Price. Pick Any Two

This mantra has been around for years. I will always remember the quality–speed–price scenario being applied to the printing business. It's a real pickle, isn't it? You are wanting some high quality business cards to represent your business. You need them now and at a good price. What is the probability of getting quality, speed and price all on the same day? Pretty low. So how do you select the two?

In multifamily acquisitions, once a strike price is reached the clock starts ticking on the due diligence phase. No matter if the deal requires a "quick closing" or is slow and involved, either way presents a limited amount of time to perform all the necessary steps to reach closing day on a date certain.

**Quality**. Sometimes it's OK to lower quality standards. Like buying an ice cream cone. Good or bad once eaten you can choose a different flavor or vendor next time. In real estate due diligence that luxury is unacceptable. With respect to title work, for example, there is never a reason to cut corners.

**Speed**. Speed can be accomplished with preparedness. Your service providers must be aligned prior to having the contract signed. Legal, title, mortgage financing, environmental, property management. All of these companies (service providers) should be ready to do their part (and obligated) on the very first day of the due diligence period. Otherwise, you are already behind.

**Price**. For legal work, as an example, we need competent counsel. Granted, every deal isn't in need of a $500 an hour real estate attorney. However, that's no reason to use an ambulance chaser on your eight million dollar deal. Common sense must prevail. There is often a correlation between price and experience. And based on the complexity of commercial transactions YOUR transaction is no place to let a new kid practice their craft; no matter the craft. Yes, it's perfectly fine having junior members on the team but they must be directly supervised by the old heads that have been on this path five hundred times before.

When it comes to the choice of "pick any two" my advice is to avoid this perspective to the best of your ability. A quality multifamily acquisition is a long–term investment with a high dollar value. Short–changing the due diligence process leaves you without defense if the items that went without review pre–closing are brought to light post–closing... all for the sake of saving a buck. It can be a very expensive dollar saved, indeed.

# Depreciation: Is Faster Always Better?

If you are familiar with my acquisitions perspective then you already know the mantra: know your exit strategy prior to acquisition. The right time to discuss your exit strategy is prior to buying any asset. Granted, things change. The point is to think about the potential "exit" during acquisition. And with that, let's talk about depreciation.

**Depreciation is an income tax deduction that allows a taxpayer to recover the cost or other basis of certain property. It is an annual allowance for the wear and tear, deterioration, or obsolescence of the property (www.irs.gov)**

As "universities" formed across Europe the course of study began with classical history to a culmination of "a man of letters" after eighteen months of study. In the U.S. we have since honed this traditional education to the modern–day four–year degree that takes many people five years to achieve.

Becoming an accountant then, anymore, requires a four–year degree along with various forms of advanced training, often leading to a second degree; a Masters in Accountancy. And then (finally) the opportunity to sit for the Certified Public Accounting designation.

Why this history? To denote the level of formal education required of accounting professionals and to point out that the profession of accounting requires serious study. These are the professionals we hire to ascertain, with a high degree of certainty, how to follow tax rules, to apply depreciation and depreciation schedules.

Many will direct their accountant to advance any potential depreciation schedule to capture as much depreciation as possible as fast as possible. We call this "accelerated depreciation."

**Accelerated depreciation is any method of depreciation used for accounting or income tax purposes that allows greater deductions in the earlier years of the life of an asset. (www.investopedia.com)**

Why do we ask for maximum utilization of accelerated depreciation? Most investors have no idea. They just know, or think they know, that faster is better. And THAT is not the right answer. The right answer is different for every investor. Owners of commercial real estate assets are a diverse bunch. From "Mom and Pop" owners to billion dollar sovereign wealth funds, the spectrum of owners and ownership structures is vast. So why think that in each and every circumstance a more rapid use of depreciation is positive?

This thinking fails to take into account individual investor investment exit strategy as well as the tax position of the investor. Outcomes for a single property investor will differ substantially from those of an investor with a large portfolio of properties. The "speed" of the underlying depreciation methods/choices can level out these inconsistencies. Also, please note the IRS does allow a "do over" as to method changes in depreciation in post–acquisition years. Therefore, when thinking depreciation strategy tailor depreciation for particular investors and property. There is no one–size–fits–all.

# Five Ways to Establish Turnover Numbers

In multifamily acquisitions the best time to think about your exit strategy is before the acquisition. The same rule applies to determining or establishing average annual turnover. What better time to look at turnover than before buying the deal?

Your objective when reviewing turnover is to identify the source: is turnover "natural" or attributed to other causes? What are these "other causes" and can these factors be addressed post closing? This discussion is under multifamily acquisitions because the best time to ascertain the state of turnover, or renewals, is pre–purchase.

The benefits to identifying the source of turnover is placing you in a position to attack the biggest offender once you own the deal. Here are some broad "brush stroke" methods for taking a look at turnover. These methods fall short of performing a 100% lease file review.

Following are five places to look for the causes, or reasoning, behind turnover. Note that the national average in multifamily is fifty percent turnover per year. Identifying the cause of turnover is no witch hunt. Finding and blaming a person or entity doesn't solve the problem.

**The Rent Roll.** Look at year–over–year changes in occupancy on a unit–by–unit basis. How many families remain on the rent roll from the prior year? What "percentage change" does this simple review suggest?

**Existing Leases**. Are existing leases in order? Do they auto–renew to a month–to–month (bad) or is a newly-signed annual lease renewal required (good)? Are the lease renewals in good order?

**The Market**. In large cities with significant competition, the market can create turnover based on competitive factors. It's a free country. People can move if they want to. Many a resident has moved to save $600 a year in rent even though the move may have costs three times that amount.

In a recent news story a retail shop in New York was closed because of complaints about the constant smell of bacon. So now we know; a market can change for reasons like jobs leaving town, higher crime, newer competition or...bacon. Who knew?

**Management Expertise**. What is your assessment of the existing management and maintenance regimen? Are they engaged? Do they have a renewal schedule that is 30, 60 or 90 days ahead of lease expiration? Is management pro–active? Can they tell you annual turnover for the last quarter or year?

**Property Dynamics**. Are there certain things about the asset that just will not or cannot be changed? Does it sit on a loud, well–traveled road? Do sixty logging trucks drive by every day at five a.m.? Is it next to an active fire station that uses sirens at all hours of the day and night?

The best thing about assessing turnover before you purchase a property is the thinking time this allows for addressing how to remedy high turnover. This is a very good use of your brain power as post–closing a plan of action can be ready for immediate implementation.

# The Secret to Buying Low and Selling High

The secret to buying low and selling high is the same secret to losing weight: time, focused attention and following a quality plan of action. Yet if this was easy, everyone would do it, right? Buying low is a relative term. Low where?

### A Plan, Time and Expertise

Making money in any business requires a plan of action, time and expertise; and you need all three to have a high degree of success. In real estate, add capital. Lots and lots of capital. Sure, you can add leverage but along with this comes the need for an increased risk appetite. Yield requirements change along the capital stack; the thinner the equity, the higher the yield requirements from an investor near the top of the capitol stack.

Assuming leverage is at an acceptable level, how long does it take to make any money in real estate? Here is my least favorite answer; that depends. No one can time the market. If they could, every real estate owner would have dumped their portfolio in 2007 and repurchased it for less. So that's out.

While you cannot time the market, you can make educated guesses about future events. For example; interest rates have been artificially low for many years. Chances are they will rise. Chances are they will rise much faster and much higher than most people believe is possible. Thus, prepare accordingly.

Back to timing. Let's stick with rental property; property that generates a monthly income. There are five ways to make money:

**Appreciation**
**Income**
**Depreciation**
**Mortgage principal reduction**
**Active management**

As an owner of real property you have no control over appreciation unless you consider market and submarket conditions prior to the buy decision. The other four categories, however, are ongoing parts of being engaged in this business.

How do you address income? Do you have good counsel for selecting how depreciation is taken? Did you select the right mortgage vehicle for long–term ownership? Are you actively managing the asset? These are all part of having a good plan of action.

Applying appropriate expertise to real property assets and given time to develop your plan will set your sail in the right direction for reaping benefits from an eventual sale. Thus, while you cannot time the market you can attempt to gauge the best time to sell an asset based on the availability of equity and debt in the marketplace at any given time.

What is the secret to buying low and selling high? There is no one secret but many facets to solving the equation for making this occur beginning with time, giving the asset your focused attention and following a quality plan of action.

# Buying Class

People within the industry have strong opinions about asset class differentiation. I'm referring to designating assets as Class A, B or C. For many institutional buyers, any deal under 200 units is considered non–institutional and therefore cannot be considered an acquisition candidate. Another easy qualifier for institutional deals is ceiling height. Assets, regardless of size, without nine foot ceilings are screened out by many corporate buyers of multifamily assets.

Class reaches beyond age and condition. It includes size, demographics, operational efficiencies, quality of construction, quality of interior and exterior finish work and rents. Following is a synopsis of multifamily assets and distinctions between A, B and C.

**Class A**. Always the newest product in the market offering the latest amenities. Offered at the highest rent per square foot. Differentiation is created by emphasizing being "best in class" and being the new kid on the block. Class A assets provide a sense of place, they represent an ambiance beyond just the address. They provide services in addition to offering a place of residence.

**Class B**. Represents various degrees of product type regarding age, but are usually well maintained and in good condition. Class B may rent for $500 or $2,500 a month depending on the market. Institutional professionals will place an age limit on Class B buildings often stating that anything over 20 years old falls out of the category. This classification narrows B assets too much because assets from Appleton to Pasadena that are substantially older represent solid B quality assets.

**Class C**. Known as "workforce housing." Workforce housing is represented by individuals and families earning between 60-120% of the median household income. It is substantially functional but with deferred maintenance apparent. Credit quality of the resident base is less than perfect and turnover is usually higher than for A and B assets. Class C fills up after lower tier Class B assets are already full. Using age as a qualifier, again, would suggest that any asset older than 30 years old is Class C. This is closer to the truth for C quality than for B quality. There are exceptions, but fewer exceptions than for Class B.

**Everything else**. Everything else are those assets that fall outside of the prior definitions. For example, when an investor purchases a C building sitting on an A location with the intention of demolition. Or, such as 1950's built duplex, a four–story walk–up in a major metro (meaning no elevators) or converted basements rented as living quarters.

Many non–institutional buyers look at assets from a market specific perspective rather than through the lens of class. Class alone does not have to be your watermark for acquisitions, but it's good to have a working knowledge of class to assist in defining competitive forces.

# What is a Rent Roll?

A rent roll, correctly assembled, is a distinctive document providing you with an array of information. When buying a rental property you are in essence buying the rent roll and the monthly income that comes with it. Why is it important to establish the amount of monthly income from the rent roll? Because this is the contractual re–occurring revenue established from existing, in–force leases. The rent roll is a snapshot of current income as represented by the owner of the asset.

**The rent roll is the property owner's representation of rental income derived from an income–producing real estate asset.**

The rent roll is the most critical document in formulating the value of income property. Authenticating numbers on the rent roll leads to creating a high level of comfort in your property buying decision–making process. When considering the acquisition of income property, without discounting the importance of various ancillary income sources, you must devote the most attention to the largest source of revenue, which is the rental income as reflected on the rent roll.

The lease file review is imperative. A review of each lease file is imperative to validating contractual rental income as reflected on the rent roll. Any number represented on the rent roll must tie to a date and amount as denoted on leases; from rent to late fees to lease term.

The rent roll is a snapshot of rents due for the period as reflected in signed and valid leases. The rent roll is utilized by owners, managers, lenders and government agencies as a springboard to understanding the value and stability of a particular real property asset. The rent roll will state the start and end date of the obligation to pay rent, per the terms of the lease.

Is it true that "if" is the biggest word in the English language? In rent roll analysis, "if" rents collected as described by executed leases matched the rent roll, month in and month out, answering the question about collected rental income is answered. Alas, this is seldom the case.

There is no room for the word "if" in due diligence on rental property acquisitions. There is too much money at stake. If (there's that word again) you are buying rental property, then the money at stake is probably yours. Therefore what you do to acknowledge and address discrepancies between rental income as presented and rental income legally due per the collective leases is vastly important.

Excerpts of this article are derived from John Wilhoit's book, How to Read a Rent Roll: A Guide to Understanding Rental Income.

# The 1031 Dog That Has Yet To Bark (Again)

You may have heard there is plenty of money in the market for real estate acquisitions. Of course, like any other urban legend the facts are a difficult thing to come by as the lens becomes more focused.

Like politics real estate is local. So, local to New York City there is a significant amount of money and property assets moving around. The same is true for most job center cities. Delineated at the transaction level the size and scope of deals trading reflect a reality that at the top and bottom of the food chain deals are moving much faster than those in the middle.

According to an article in National Real Estate Institute (NREI) there were $4.1 Billion dollars in 1031 exchanges in 2007. In 2010 that number was $1 Billion dollars. Transaction volume is nowhere near pre–recession peak volume.

The United States has an improving economy, a stable housing market yet small commercial multifamily transaction volume (deals under $5M) is abruptly lower than many expect given that stabilizing operations are the rule of the day. Why? Because 1031 tax exchanges drive a HUGE percentage of these transactions. Lower 1031 activity equals lower overall activity.

In the best of times 1031 exchanges in certain markets account for as much as 30% of property trades. With tighter bank financing and lower capital gains rates 1031 money is less of a factor in overall property sales volume. But don't count it out. Every billion dollars that 1031's account for is a billion dollars in transactions that may not have occurred otherwise.

Watch the 1031 volume in your local marketplace as a marker of sales activity. Regardless of which side of the trade you are on its good to know if this tool in your toolbox is readily in use.

# Chapter 2

## Property Management

# Budgeting and the Beginner's Mind

Steve Jobs had an affinity for Zen. One of the concepts he deployed in business was "the beginners mind." In its most basic form "the beginners mind" allows us to believe that in any circumstance there are many possibilities. Interesting. Can we apply this to the annual budgeting process for our assets?

The over–simplified budgeting process: take last year's budget, compare it with actual, split the differences and add 3% to revenue categories and 2% to expense categories. Done. Next! So much for thoughtfulness, professionalism or being connected to reality. Budgeting can be a "value add" proposition, assisted by the beginners mind perspective.

## In Any Circumstance there are Many Possibilities

Annual budgeting must take into account the realities of each asset; the physical asset and its market. A picture perfect asset with 300 newly built units across the street in a market with slow absorption has to factor in the impact of the new competition. These factors should be reflected in the budget.

Tony Golsby–Smith wrote a blog for Harvard Business Review entitled "Is Your Budgeting Process Killing Your Strategy" (http://blogs.hbr.org/cs/2011/01/is_your_budgeting_process_kill.html). This thought shines an entirely different light on the budgeting process. While it is important to work through the minutia of asset–specific budgeting, this process must also take into account effects on the larger organization.

How do we accomplish this? With the beginners mind; by believing that in any circumstance there are many possibilities. Static number crunching that entails moving last year's actuals into next years column precludes original thought. The originality necessary in this process is taking current market dynamics into consideration during the budgeting process.

This view may require utilizing additional facets of your existing "suites" software, or re–deploying marketing savings into customer premiums to gain retention. Or, taking savings from utility usage reductions and deploying these dollars into staff training with measurable results.

Consider the annual budgeting process as more than a perfunctory, number crunching exercise. There is more to this than making assumptions and passing them up the food chain. Thinking of budgeting as a "value add" process makes the entire endeavor much more exciting, and potentially much more profitable.

# What Google and Intel Know About Real Estate Investing

What Google and Intel know about real estate investing is that a certain cross section of skills is necessary to optimally run a business. Using a fine point pen, these two global, multi–billion dollar companies have identified the necessary core competencies they desire. They know exactly the type of people they wish to hire. I believe that property management companies hiring people with these same skills could see exponential increases in productivity.

Google and Intel have scholarship competitions to encourage young people in science, engineering and computer science. Do you know a burgeoning scientist? Google and Intel are searching the globe for talented young minds to change the world.

Yet while ideals are important, the people they seek must have certain cognitive and social skills to fit into their respective organizations. Hermits need not apply. Here are few excerpts from Google's science fair site, http://www.google.com/events/sciencefair/:

*The Google Science Fair is an online science competition seeking curious minds from the four corners of the globe. Anybody and everybody between 13 and 18 can enter. All you need is an idea. Geniuses are not always A–grade students. We welcome all mavericks, square–pegs and everybody who likes to ask questions.*

In recent years the applicants at Intel's Science Research Fair attained a balance of 50/50 men and women. For the first time ever this year's competition had three women finalist. http://www.intel.com/about/corporateresponsibility/education/isef/index.htm

*The Intel International Science and Engineering Fair, a program of Society for Science & the Public, is the world's largest pre–college science fair competition. Each year, approximately seven million high school students around the globe compete in local science fairs*

*where they get the opportunity to apply classroom learning in the real world, conduct authentic research, and explore their potential as future scientists and innovators.*

What does this have to do with real estate investing? There are specific attributes these companies look for in new hires. Both companies hire people from around the world representing every time zone and dozens of countries.

What are the knowledge, skills and abilities Google and Intel are seeking in their future scientists and engineers that we can apply to property management? They are:

**Extraction** – taking a problem and presenting it in a way that allows people to work towards a solution.

**Working with Data** – skill in collecting relevant information from the ocean of information noise around us.

**Social interaction – teamwork.** Skill a and b (above) has value only when shared, thus, having the ability to work with others is essential. Teamwork is a necessary component for working on projects and problems when team members are spread across the globe.

These same skills; extraction, working with data and teamwork, are necessary for operating a successful property management business.

The connection between the talents sought by Google and Intel and property management is that being a successful real estate investor requires the successful implementation of sound property management that includes certain cognitive abilities and teamwork.

Hiring property management talent with abilities in extraction, working with data and teamwork is a solid footing for growing a great organization.

# Capturing Rent Growth

In multifamily operations rent growth is the most important component to increasing Net Operating Income (NOI). It is more important than incremental cost controls, more important than increases to Other Income. Rent growth is the line item that keeps on giving– profits. Projecting rent growth is part science, part qualitative. There are many service providers willing to assist property managers in keeping up to date on rents within a circle of competitors.

There is a caveat' however; the smaller the market the more you (the property manager) are on your own. It will be a long time until major service providers fill in to markets under 200,000 persons. In these markets the best source of intelligence is your local network of property managers, business associates and vendors. Want to know who is selling the most cheese in the local pizza restaurant wars? Ask the cheese vendor!

First and foremost is keeping current residents in place with advanced planning. Renewals, renewals, renewals. Yes, I know saying "advanced planning" is in the same category as the phrase "past experience." This is one time when the saying sticks. Here are three ways to capture rent growth.

1. **Planning ahead.** Planning for renewals is a primary methodology of capturing rent growth and maintaining stable occupancy. The more advanced the better. Ninety days is no longer an uncommon management planning timeline for contacting residents about renewing their lease.

2. **Non–cash concessions.** Utilize non–cash concessions at renewal. From restaurant gift cards to cleaning carpets and updating light fixtures; these are all potential concessions to consider at renewal. The concession offered should be less

than the additional rent captured in the rental increase over the next twelve months.

3. **Technology and Software.** Check out Multifamily Biz www. multifamilybiz.com. This website really has a great focus on technology. YieldStar www.yieldstar.com is one of many software programs that focus their outputs on maximizing income. There are others. These systems are often referred to as revenue enhancement models. Some are scalable, some are not. Choose one that you believe will more than pay for itself in terms of generating increased revenue for your assets.

# Five Rental Revenue Growth Strategies

Every operator wants rent growth. Rent growth, rent growth, rent growth. Ok, ok, ok. I understand. Year over year rent growth is the most important driver of revenue growth. How do you get it?

1. **Renewals.** Always at the top of the list. Nothing keeps income ticking like retaining in–place residents. Start the renewal process early. Recognize this as your number one tool for maintaining stabilized occupancy.

2. **Resident screening.** Our customers make or break our business. Set your standards, stick to your standards. The "great recession" created the need for some changes in credit underwriting but not so much as to bend past the point of reasonableness.

3. **Expand "other income."** If your other income revenue includes only application, late and pet fees there is room for expansion. Storage, services, cable revenue sharing, parking (premium parking spaces). Do some brainstorming to see what works best for your assets.

4. **Resident referrals.** Are you offering existing customers an incentive to bring in their friends and co–workers? Resident referrals are a cost effective method to create an opportunity to have satisfied customers introduce your property to new customers.

5. **Email.** Do you email your customers and potential customers? Oh no! Not another task! An email as often as only once a month can assist in maintaining name recognition. It's just one more place to keep your name in front of your customers. That's why Nike pays and pays to have their "swoosh" on every moving object possible. We use the Aweber email management system.

# Five Easy Crazy Cost Cutting Strategies

Let's just say you are already overworked, understaffed and touching the limits of a stretched budget with your multifamily assets. As the comedian Ron White opines: "Let's just say." Now what? What do I have to add to my already overflowing, brimming plate? Hopefully, a few things that will lighten the load by freeing up some dollars and, eventually, staff time.

**Sustainable landscaping**. Landscaping is an asset. It gives character to a place and makes it distinct, often pleasurable. But overgrowth can be unsightly and costly. One, as a negative attribute, and two, as a money/water/labor waster. It can be fun cutting stuff down, but there is more to sustainable landscaping than just getting out the chainsaws (safety glasses required here). Sometimes the value proposition is simply maintaining current top soil efficiently (read eliminating erosion).

Right–sizing landscaping is utilizing your grounds budget to increase value; aesthetic value, visual value. Here is a quote from University of Minnesota Sustainable Landscaping Urban Design Information Series: "The key to creating a sustainable landscape is understanding that the design process should be considered first. Another website with good information is Sustainable Landscape Designs.

**Real estate tax and Utility Bill Auditing**. Check it out. Really. Without a qualifier statement like; our company is too small, too big, our buildings are too old, etc. Perform an audit of utilities paid by the the property– all of them; trash pick up, telephones, water/sewer, electric.

Utility bill auditing services are very fragmented and I am unaware of an industry leader to recommend. For real estate tax auditing services stay local. Start with your accountancy firm and request a referral with this specialized expertise.

**Tech. Real High Tech**. Technology is another tool you can use to cut costs, the key is to find a provider that can actually point to something they deliver that will help reduce costs. Technology platform provider *365 Connect* is one company that knows the industry well. Since 2003, they have exclusively served the multifamily industry, winning a mountain of technology awards along the way. They target the resident life–cycle; this is where expense and revenue intersect. They built a true marketing machine that syndicates leasing data to high traffic housing search engines, social media and classified sites, all from your own community branded website, which works on any device (desktop, mobile, tablets).

What is really cool about their platform is every piece integrates with social media, eliminating redundant log–ins. They deliver a cost effective bundled package for less than you will pay one listing service. This platform reduces online marketing spend, but it cuts labor costs through pure automation. Be sure to visit the *365 Connect* website.

**Water flows**. Clean All Gutters – for real. And down spouts. Check to assure every gutter has a splash board directing water away from the building. Depending on the size of the development this could be a one hour or one day job. Small item, but with a payoff in the long run. Inspect gutters and spouts for functionality and to make sure they are securely attached. The Inspectapedia website is all about building and environmental inspections.

**Each one, teach one**. What is our biggest asset? Our people. Nothing better than an in–house mentoring program to "connect" our best people with leaders inside the company. The benefits far out–weigh the costs. This goes beyond cross–training. Mentoring allows for the up–and–comer's to be dipped in the knowledge of senior management.

The cost–cutting is derived from having a single–voice message across all channels. This one–on–one guidance of senior management being instilled into the next generation of leaders is priceless. Where is the costs savings here? In reduced staff turnover, higher staff buy–in to the message and the genuine feeling of inclusion of in–place staff.

Maybe I have stretched by stating these concepts as being "easy." Each one requires an initial investment of time to consider their viability for your circumstances. However, if any one of these ideas meets the test and can be implemented, I submit that the long term benefits will out–weigh their costs.

# Collecting Rent

Recent Resident story: "I'm in the parking lot at the grocery store and a parking spot comes open right in front! I swerve in and, at the very last moment, slam on my brakes. There is a goat tied to a shopping cart right in front of me. A goat! Right there! I get out my car and untie the goat and put it my car. Where do you take a goat in the city? Anyway, I go in the grocer to get a few things and I come back to find the goat in the front seat of my car chewing up an envelope. My rent money! Its gone. The goat ate my rent money."

Being in this business long enough will allow you to experience the greatest story telling in the world. People are creative. Ghosts appear. Tooth fairies steal. Robbers wearing track shoes. Of course, it's all funny after the fact. Part of our role is seeing the smoke from the fire. More importantly, we have a business to run. This business requires collecting funds from customers to pay expenditures, including our PM fees, and delivering proceeds to asset owners. Rental revenue runs our businesses.

An important part of rent collections is remaining consistent and refraining from any form of favoritism. If rent is due on the first and late after the fifth, then everyone paying after the fifth is assessed late fees. If the evictions policy is notification on the tenth, then this notification schedule applies equally to all.

We have found the dividing line squarely rests on communication. Residents who communicate provide us with cause, occasionally, to stray from the lock step structure of payment receipts. Along with this is the timing of said communication.

Whether the story includes farm animals or dollars melded together from roasting marshmallows, these stories seldom assist in getting our vendors paid. But they certainly can add some color to our day. But keep your eye on the prize; 100% collections, each month, every month.

# Multifamily Vacancy: 10 Negatives

When significant multifamily vacancy becomes an issue it is because of one of three reasons: the people, the paper or the property. High vacancy means one of these three have gone for a walk. And we already know paper and property are unable to walk... The people can be either ownership or management. The paper refers to implemented systems or mortgage matters. And the property, well, the property is a reflection of the people in charge.

To maintain the physical and financial health of an asset extended vacancy requires a property specific game plan. Here is a starter list of things that go south with extended vacancy:

**Asset valuation.** For all the reasons below, vacancy deteriorates asset value more severely than any other category save legal battles. Whither we shed a tear or stand and fight? Vacancy is an affront to valuation. Extended vacancy is a piercing sword to soft tissue; it cannot withstand the blade.

**Loss of revenue (of course).** Like a cruise ship, at the end of the day, the day is done. That cabin (or unit) can never recapture the opportunity to earn income from the day that has passed. Days vacant, on a property–wide basis can add up to years of lost revenue. Ten vacant units for 30 days equals 300 days of vacancy!!!

**Intensive staff time.** With extensive vacancy your property management staff is devoting their energies to a remedy. This requires other noteworthy management tasks to be pushed back or eliminated until the vacancy issue is addressed.

**Utility costs.** Want to lose lots of money real fast? Heat and cool vacant units for an extended period. I can hear the sucking sound from here...

**Upkeep. Stuff happens.** Like neglect or a slow water leak that goes unnoticed. With significant vacancy priorities get re–ordered.

Without HVAC being monitored or toilet leaks addressed a small problem can turn into a much larger one.

**Neglecting newly vacated units.** This is bad on many fronts; first, that newly vacated unit may be an easy turn. Or worse, food and other matters remain with the utilities off. Worse still, there could be fleas, these are things that cannot/should not wait for a week or three. The need to get product rented could mean that recent vacants are lost in the shuffle, without a walk–through, without an immediate clean. Note to staff: walk every vacant unit with delivery of keys.

**Neglected long–standing vacant units.** Physical deterioration in an empty unit can sometimes be subtle, sometimes overt. How do you know? Can you document the last time a staff member walked into each vacant unit? Are there notes on what they found? If the answer is no to all of the above, then neglect is presently occurring.

**Advertising costs and monitoring.** No matter your advertising type, increases in vacancy require increased attention to advertising. And someone has to monitor the results. Who is in charge? Is advertising and lead follow up addressed by someone who is fully aware of the urgency?

**Pride, Desperation and Blame.** Owners, property managers, Regional Managers, sometimes start the blame game. At the point in time when focus should be on "what" (the what being vacancy) much hot air is wasted pointing fingers. Granted, this is sometimes a necessary exercise to determine weak points. But once determined, get the train going, get the resources working on eliminating the issue.

**The costs side (back to valuation).** With fewer occupied units and less revenue, fixed and variable costs are a higher percentage of gross revenue. This fact decreases real and perceived market value.

The extended cost of vacancy is reflected in low valuation. We work to make money, earning equity with our expertise, letting time carry value via improved operations, rental increases and a reduction in debt. Long–term vacancy affects all of these.

If current management is unable to address the matter, find new management. If you are self–managing multifamily and performance is sub–par, then fire yourself and seek professional management. Interview several companies for fit with the skill set to address the immediate vacancy issue and transition to stabilized operations. Time is of the essence!

# Multifamily and Crime

From Perry Mason to CSI (Los Angeles, New York and Miami– what a franchise) and Law & Order, as a society we are intrigued by violence while concurrently trying to avoid it in our own lives. The issue is that crime does not always happen to someone else. It can impact you, your family, your residents, your assets.

If you are in any way involved with income property management then sometime during your career path you and the assets under your management will be impacted by crime. Sometimes, violent crime.

I am not exactly sure why crime is such a big seller on television. There are more Cops and Robber shows than ever. Perhaps it is because even a single act of crime impacts so many lives. When crime comes to your doorstep it is usually unexpected and seldom perpetrated by residents. People forget that criminals have cars too. They are mobile.

On LinkedIn®, there is a group, "Property Management Professionals." One of the threads is specific to all matters related to property management and crime. It is called Crime and Security. It is a place where you will learn more than one new thing about the subject. "You must be signed in to LinkedIn® to access Property Management Professionals thread and the Crime and Security thread."

What I am about to say is an oversimplification, but I am going to say it anyway. To the best of your ability, avoid turning a blind eye to criminal activity. We all have a 'self–preservation" instinct that says "DON'T GET INVOLVED." I'm not suggesting throwing yourself in the middle of a gun fight. But call the authorities even anonymously. Leaving it to someone else means it doesn't get done. Who knows how many lives a single phone call may save.

# The Case for Strategic Vacancy

Why create vacancy? Strategic vacancy is always planned and has a purpose; that purpose is increasing rents.

Rent is not always about price; we provide a service and our customers are looking for a comfortable place, a peaceable place to reside. If everyone in your market is at the exact same price point, then your potential customers will gravitate to the place they perceive provides the most value at that price.

The "differentiation" you create can sometimes include nothing more than color or freshness. Other times the changes are more overt like new...everything. Most times these changes are something in between. Tracking changes in rents in the market in real–time allows management to ascertain rental increases from implemented upgrades.

Once the revenue gap between current rents in "as is" units is measured against potential rents with "upgrades" you have established cause to consider creating vacancy to capture this gap between current rents and potential rent with upgrades. The bigger the gap, the more cause to consider upgrades.

**Preparing for rent growth**

Are you using tools of the trade to see rent growth in your markets and submarkets? Are managers performing rent surveys to keep pace with competitive assets? Are your concessions and/or premiums attracting the right customer to your assets? Preparing for rent growth requires a yes response to all of these questions. Without knowing these simple market dynamics  you have no idea about pending rent growth and your assets will miss these gains.

Can you see rent growth coming in your market? If the answer is yes then consider creating  strategic vacancy in advance  to prepare to capture this wave of cash. Is this a serious statement? Absolutely. Owners do it all the time. Following are a few examples.

**Creating vacancy on purpose...**

**Asset renovation.** Renovation is a relative word. We can renovate individual units and entire complexes. We can tear down to the studs or pick up and replace all the common area floor coverings. Renovation for rent growth can take on any of these facets. Renovation can be minor or major with the presumption that the greater the renovation the greater the anticipated increase in rental revenue from improvements. Ah, but there is that word– presumption. No one is spending a few hundred thousand (or more) based on presumption. That is why we establish potential rental increases and tie this number to potential renovation items.

**Asset Repositioning**. Repositioning may or may not include a renovation piece. The repositioning can be a cosmetic facelift to the facade or property entry points or lots of grass seed, flowers and shrubs. Repositioning can be exclusively marketing or rebranding an asset to take advantage of certain market dynamics.

**Removal of low quality customers.** You seldom remove existing residents based on what is in their credit file. Sometimes you take a risk, right? You allow a person to move in who does not fit your rental profile from a credit history perspective. If you vary from your own established standards then there will be problems.

Then, down the road, we purposefully create vacancy to remove these same problematic residents (a problem we created). We notify of nonrenewal at the end of the initial lease term. The objective of creating a vacant unit is to reduce staff time having to address chronically slow paying residents. In this example, even if the unit were rented to another at the same rental rate as the resident we have asked to leave you have gained efficiency because of having reduced staff time necessary to pursue collections. Thus, the vacancy you created will increase rental revenue based on receipt of timely payments going forward.

Whether renovation, repositioning or lifting credit quality, you can see there are sometimes good reasons to create vacancy that will lead to increasing the value of your assets. Each strategy requires a well thought out  time  horizon and quality planning; operationally and fiscally. Each strategy requires its own budget forecast taking into account dips to income during and after implementation.

# Disrupting *Vacuam* (Vacancy)

V*acuam* is Latin for empty space. In the property management business we live and breathe around occurrences of empty space. Reality is that empty space is "non–revenue" producing. And since our fixed costs of operations revolves around revenue generation, eliminating vacancy is the best method for increasing revenue.

How do we disrupt vacancy? Prior to disrupting vacancy you have to know where it's coming from. The first order of business is to determine the source of vacancy.

**Vacancy/Source.** Is the issue with credit quality or some other factor? Are residents remaining for the entire term of their lease or leaving early? If leaving early, why? Is maintenance being addressed timely or never? Are there competitive assets offering super incentives? Has street traffic increased or decreased significantly in recent months?

**Average Vacancy.** What are the average number of days vacant monthly for each asset you manage? How long is a newly vacated unit vacant? What is your turn time? Are you prepared for vacancy as it occurs?

**Aggregate Vacancy.** Here is the scary number that you must know: how many days vacant at each asset each month multiplied by the most recent twelve months? Is this number 100? Is it 1,000? Multiply this number by the average revenue per unit per day and this provides the vacancy loss number in dollars.

Granted, this is the tip of the larger vacancy iceberg as we haven't added in concessions, evictions in process, renovations and off–line units. Starting with vacancy source, reviewing average and aggregate vacancy will point you towards areas of concern allowing management to align action steps against the biggest offenders.

# Amplifying the Positive

Name three things that are outstanding about your real estate assets. The three things that came to mind first, were they benefits or features? People like features but they buy benefits. This is a sincere question– what are the benefits to the end user? Ok, shelter. Check. Every competitor offers this benefit. What else? Are you amplifying the positives? Are you communicating your competitive advantages?

Did you have to think hard on this or were these positive attributes just flowing automatically? How about the on–site staff? Can they name impressive attributes with only a few mis–placed um's? As advocates for your assets there is no better person to accentuate the positives.

Think beyond carpet and paint. Even the oldest, smallest quarters have some positives. Bay windows, perhaps. Close proximity to public transit and a good local deli. Trees, plants, flowers! Landscaping can really contribute to the feel of a place.

Also, note that in any organization your biggest asset is people. Who is picking up the phone? Are they a help or hindrance to solving resident request? I recall reading that one of the most startling phone calls the president of Hertz Rental Car ever made was to his own office and the ensuing treatment he received. When was the last time you called your properties?

Positives can be something other than physical attributes that make your property great. For example, consistent service is a real attribute. Things like immediate response to maintenance or that grounds and common areas are spotless.

Perhaps your multifamily property offers flexible lease terms with price differentials based on term. Benefits can be something other than new carpet (although that never hurts). My point is to think inside the box (about what is in the actual unit) and outside the box (everything else; from ambiance to proximity of medical services).

# Carpet, Tile, Vinyl and Wood

As property managers, we spend more real cash on flooring that just about any other item. Excluding roofs, windows and boilers, flooring is often the one line item expenditure that pops on the annual profit/loss. Some property managers are flooring experts. Most people muddle forward executing a flooring strategy that needs work.

With flooring, there is always the necessary balance between initial costs and longevity. Frankly, as you know, it's sometimes a crap shoot based on how hard people live in a unit. But irrespective of the covering we are generally choosing from four options: Carpet, wood, tile or vinyl.

Excluding seasonal and tropical adjustments most people have a preference for carpet. Preference or not, let's look at some alternative flooring types.

Which flooring is best? Part of the answer depends on use, weather and location. Consider for this writing we are discussing garden apartment interiors with normal turnover.

**Carpet.** Ye olde standby. Always there, always versatile. Tremendous selection and quality choices. A must–use material on second and third floor living area interiors (living rooms in particular).

Now that carpet pad is approaching the same price point as carpet, consider using eight pound (8 lb) pad. It adds longevity, bounce and is easier for installers to work (they love it compared to 6 lb).

Manufacturer direct can work well with carpet, but even here it's necessary to have a very clear understanding of product specifications. For example: ordering three hundred yards of "oak leaf" carpet requires that the entire delivered product is from the same exact production run to assure 100% color match. Accepting delivery of two 150 yard rolls from separate production runs may leave you with two similar, but different colors.

**Wood**. There is wood (actual wood from trees machined into wood flooring) and there is "wood finish" tile. Which are you looking for wood or wood finish? Either is wonderful to have in the leasing showroom and high traffic common areas that have daily attention. Wood is a great product with stellar longevity but often priced beyond usefulness in garden apartments unless rents are approaching $2 a square foot.

**Tile**. I am a big fan of tile. Heavily used in the south based on warm year–round temperatures. Longevity is the real selling point. Don't get fancy with it as we want this type of installed flooring to "fit" ten and fifteen years out. Earth tones and basic colors– those that cover stains.

Use grout with some color as white will require more maintenance over time. Other than the occasional crack or because of abuse tile is a better buy than carpet or wood. Slightly higher costs per square foot going in but a much better return on investment over the long–term.

Find a local professional to learn the best choice for your location. The vocabulary here is huge. We say "tile" a professional says...

- Ceramic
- Porcelain
- Saltillo (Spanish tile)
- Terracotta (baked earth)
- Terrazzo (marble, granite and concrete)

**Vinyl**. Laminates have their place. When installed right with the correct under–layment, it is long–lasting and easy to replace when necessary. Good for kitchens, bathrooms, laundry rooms and entryways.

**Brick**. Yes, I said brick. It may just fit in certain circumstances so consider this as just one more potential material. It's more likely that a "brick finish" will be the end result over concrete (see concrete below).

**Concrete**. In some common areas concrete can be suitable depending on climate. There are numerous methods for making plain concrete into good looking, livable space.

- Textured or Stampable
- Stenciled toppings
- Stained, dyed or polished

**Mix n' Match**

Can you mix and match materials? Of course. One of the things we like to do with two–story townhomes is use a tile product on the upstairs landing. It's a one–time install and going forward any carpet replacement is only in bedrooms. We never have to touch the landing again. Yes, it's $300 vs. $75 for carpet, but it is done forever. Makes no sense if your company buys/sells rapidly. Makes a lot of sense if you are a long–term owner.

Consider using "25 year" product (tile, concrete) in any high traffic areas where the costs factor is justified. There are commercial grade flex–tile products that claim to have a 20 year life (like those installed in the clothing section of your local Wal–Mart– they should know).

We have devoted little space to carpet here even though it is the main–stay staple product. That's because it is so well known. Our focus in this writing is to get you thinking about cost effective alternatives that add variety, longevity and differentiation to your multifamily assets.

# How to Select a Lock

This is a discussion on selecting door locks for apartment communities. Having this conversation ten years ago our consensus was that early in the 21st century we would all have paperless offices and keyless locks. Guess what; didn't happen. Is your office paperless? Are your communities keyless? The likelihood is low.

Electronic locks are the future. They provide a myriad of benefits to commercial multifamily property owners. New developments with on–site management must consider the benefits of electronic locks. But then there is everyone else; those with assets new and old that have 100 year–old technology (older really)– the lock and key.

Many multifamily communities fall into one of two categories; one lock per door or two locks per door. Surprisingly, safety is seldom the determinant. The decision on locks–per–door was decided by the builder or architect. The developer selected one lock as a costs conscious action. The architect looks at functionality and "design." Read anything about safety in this description? Nope.

Locks represent the ultimate "weakest link" theory, whereas, the weakest link is always the first to break down. As property manager, it is your job to strengthen any and all weak systems. The beginning point for selecting locks is to perform an assessment of the in–place lock and safety systems. Are they appropriate, are they functional considering the multifamily assets and the placement of the asset within the community?

**Are Keys Secure?**

The first order of business is to know without question the whereabouts of every master key. One lost master key can mean thousands of dollars in rekeying expenses.

- Is there a schedule for checking the whereabouts of master keys?

- Are they accounted for when there is personnel turnover?

- Are master keys stamped with "do not duplicate?"

- Are individual unit keys (extra keys and those for vacants) under lock?

**Do they work?**

Locks are like the heat shield system on the Space Shuttle– they either work or they don't. There is no second chance when put to the test. Granted, locks are not designed to withstand an assault on the entire entryway. But they should function as a deterrent to easy entry by unknown parties.

**Select a Uniform Brand**

When selecting locks aim for uniformity in quality and brand. Larger properties, or property management companies, will have equipment for rekeying onsite or at a central maintenance facility so it just makes sense to utilize a single make and model. This is also a step towards controlling expenses when implemented. The initial costs will have a positive return on investment for long–term owners.

Locks and keys are an operational area where the low cost bid could be a negative. Consider buying a third–party opinion from a locksmith; have a locksmith perform an assessment for a flat fee. You may be surprised at the findings.

# Six Ways to Buy a Kitchen Appliance

Scale. The real issue with any capital expenditure is scale. With respect to appliances for multifamily, do you know your annual expenditures on a property-by-property basis? If the answer is yes, then buying options are easier to qualify. Real estate investing is best accomplished with economies of scale. Buying power for appliance purchases is one of many examples.

In a stabilized multifamily property everyday appliances include stoves, dishwashers, refrigerators and microwaves (built in). Unlike disposals and locks, unless there is secure storage on site, keeping reserve appliances on hand is seldom a good idea. It's amazing how often a refrigerator can "grow legs" if left un–attended for several months. Here are a few options for just–in–time appliances.

**Buying refurbished appliances.** Refurbished electric or gas stoves can be a good buy. There are few moving parts and replacement parts are easy to come by. For all other appliances going the used route is much more difficult. Refrigerators have a mind of their own once moved around a few times and determining age is sometimes difficult. Microwaves and dishwashers are just too inexpensive brand new considering the labor involved for install.

**Home Depot vs. Lowes**. Tomato, tomato; pick your vegetable. When prices are similar it is the people that make the difference. Stick with stores that provide you with the best service, selection and price– in that order. Great prices without good people backing it up has higher costs in the end.

**Bulk purchase from manufacturer**. With appropriate credit accounts established, GE will deliver right to your door. Most manufacturers have specific credit and volume requirements to assure their major retail outlets remain competitive. In other words, selling direct to you has to make business sense without undercutting their bread and butter resale customers.

**Local Appliance Supplier**. They have great buying power on the local front. In most circumstances they can procure better pricing from the OEM (Original Equipment Manufacturer) than you can. Give them a chance. Sometimes the best deal is right under our nose.

**Mail Order/Drop shipper/Direct from Manufacturer**. Using distant product providers requires strong operators and strong relationships. The issue is returns and shipping; the hassle factor for returns and the costs of shipping. Best used for parts rather than full, free standing appliances. Can work out well for small orders of boxed goods or with new construction.

**Auction Houses**. All sales final. Buy at your own risk. Kind of like "Storage Wars" your purchase is of unknown quality. Even "new in the box" purchases can have damage.

# Mowing the Grass

You have seen those commercials in the dead of winter showing sunny beaches and in summer months the polar opposite; snowy peaks. Well, this writing is like those commercials.

Landscaping is important. In property management, spring is when we set up for the summer pool season. Winter is the time to think about the spring growing season and how to best address grounds maintenance. Addressing landscaping, ground cover, plantings and soils seems like such a simple question. At the very least it takes pre–planning to assure fixed price contracts in advance of service.

If a plant scientist were to survey the grounds of your income property assets their report might say: there are 55 "species" of plants and three invasive varietals negatively impacting sustainability. And your comment would be, "I only want my property to look good, neat and clean with green grass and pretty flowers. What's all this talk about invasive species!"

Like farming, property management requires having a well rounded skill set. Alas, we must rely on our subject matter experts to get us through the necessary gory details. For example, using the wrong seed in shady areas can be a flat out waste of money. The use of plants that require high maintenance should be avoided when a suitable substitute with lower carry costs is appropriate. Factor in water conservation. Some plants truly drink like elephants.

The importance of ground cover in landscaping really comes into play when the conversation includes any word similar to soils erosion or basement leaks. When it comes to soil conservation, preservation and removing or redirecting runoff we want ground cover to be our friend. This requires planning.

Too many people think of grounds as exclusively a cost center vs. an asset to preserve. For grounds work the two options available to most income property owners are self–service or contract. For commercial assets there is nothing wrong with having dedicated staff for grounds if this fits within the larger budget.

I caution you to make sure the landscaping line item never becomes a jobs program whereas staff is mowing three times a week to look busy. Like Professor Drucker taught us with just–in–time inventory management, sometimes contract providers can be far and away the best and most costs effective solution.

# Top 10 Worst Property Management Mistakes

The question that will come to mind as you read this is "who does that?" The unfortunate answer is too many people. We are in an industry full of talented people. Mostly.

If these mistakes are occurring with your assets it is probably time to look for new management, first to stop the damage and second to remedy the potential of on–going issues and the exposure they present. Suffice to say these are all ..... bad.

**1. Allowing a danger to public safety to persist.** Suspect electrical, known illegal drug use, endangerment of children, domestic abuse, violent behavior. No good choices here. All or any similar issues must be addressed in real time once known.

**2. Creating, encouraging or allowing fraudulent acts.** No one should be skimming off the top. PM is a business. If you cannot operate the business without a very high level of integrity then get out of the business, please.

**3. Keeping a bad hire.** Other than fire or natural disasters, keeping a bad hire is one of the costliest mistakes. It is one thing to make the mistake, quite another to allow it to persist and potentially cause more damage.

**4. Bad resident screening (or no resident screening).** Anymore, the expense of obtaining a background screening is really, really cheap insurance. Having this tool available and failing to implement is trouble waiting to happen.

**5. Letting water run.** Indoors. Outdoors. Running water is seldom a positive. Find the pliers. Call the plumber, the roofer, the candlestick maker– whoever has the answer. Get that water stopped. Same day.

**6. Allowing insurance to lapse.** 'nough said. Murphy's Law lives here.

**7. Ignoring maintenance calls.** News flash; they do not go away. Good will is hard to earn, easy to lose. If management doesn't care about your customers who will?

**8. Ignoring renewals.** The number one objective to retaining a stable income stream is making sure your customers are staying with a proactive renewal policy. No renewals policy, no stable income.

**9. Lack of recordkeeping.** Uncle Sam eventually catches up and when he does it's like an ocean wave hitting a single piece of sand. Keep good records. File tax documents on time using quality service providers.

**10. Avoiding the telephone.** Telephone etiquette and responsiveness is important. Implement a policy and stick with it. Your customers and potential customers want consistency. Having the attitude of "they'll call back" is self–deception.

**10(a). Unavailability of Product** (as commented by Vicki Sharp). "Having empty units with none available to show is an obvious candidate for being one of the seven deadly sins in property management. Livable space is our product. Having this livable space in condition for showing to potential paying customers is why property owners hire property managers. Granted, this sets financial considerations aside.

**10(b). Lowering credit standards** (as commented by Mark Dewey). "Reducing credit qualification standards during the application process provides an immediate bump to occupancy but at too high a cost. Reducing credit standards creates a "downward" spiral as collections and other similar activity increases. Basically, you are taking product off–line only to see average revenue per unit decrease."

**10(c). Under estimating preventative maintenance costs** (as commented by Terry Graves). Property managers under estimate the need to do monthly and quarterly preventative maintenance.

# The Elements of Heat, Ice and Water

Weather affects every property differently. I've seen buildings side–by–side where wind completely removed one roof while leaving the building next door intact. The elements like heat (fire), snow, water and ice take a terrible toll on property assets. They are a constant, never-ending source of pressure that can only be deflected, but never fully removed.

Heat, ice and water are the three constant weather elements affecting your real estate. Each asset standing today that is still standing in 30 years will have survived almost 11,000 days of weather.

Here is something we can all agree on; 30 years from now every property in operation will be 30 years older. Such a simple statement, yes? Unfortunately it is untrue. Some assets will have been demolished. Other assets will be younger than their actual years because of redevelopment or substantial rehabilitation.

One major reason for the variance in useful life is the effect of weather and the quality of building materials (weather appropriate) used in construction.

Consider a new roof with picture perfect maintenance. Still, the life of this particular major capital expenditure is 20–25 years. This precludes damage from wind, hail or manmade gaffs.

**Heat** (heat from the sun) naturally breaks down every chemical known to man over time. This includes roofing, any sealant in use (around windows, caulking in baths and kitchens), rubberized waterline en–casements, flooring.

**Ice.** Ice, as they say, is a law suit waiting to happen. Like certain family members, you can't stop them from showing up and hope they only stay for a short while.

**Water.** Water tends to find it's way into the smallest cracks and freeze again (expanding small cracks). There is seldom a seasonal break from H2O.

In an attempt to direct water to flow where we choose, we build storm drains, washouts, breaker walls, waterways, culverts. And yet water still takes a toll as even this infrastructure requires maintenance to assure that water runs where directed. In some instances, once water finds its path it can be near impossible to divert.

The best thing to do about weather is be proactive in affected areas (interior and exterior) in an effort to stay one step ahead. Sometimes this is simple, like having working gutters. Other times hard, like when the snow budget is blown to pieces by a hard winter. No matter the season, you cannot ignore weather's effects or escape the cost of addressing the elements.

# Property Management and the Rule of Law

There are people in every community who believe the rule of law applies to everyone except them. Many are desensitized to violence and intimidation based on continuous exposure to these behaviors.

Property managers work diligently on retaining paying customers. However, there are some customers that must be removed from the property irrespective of their payment history– those who do not respect the rule of law.

Who wants to remove a resident with a good payment record? For the greater good this is sometimes necessary. Once revealed, criminal activity of any kind cannot be allowed to continue. Disclaimer: for the finer points in your municipality seek local counsel.

Too many people live in fear, real fear, afraid to ask for help. And not just the elderly. Although we cannot control the world around us we can and should, to the best of our abilities, help those than cannot help themselves.

Must do phone calls to places like child protective services, elderly care and for threats to the public from those with mental health issues.

The big gray area is expressed in terms like intimidation, scary or uncomfortable. Hardly quantifiable, but real all the same to those who bring such concerns to your attention.

People can and do change over time. A long–time resident may have recently had involvement in criminal or drug-related activity that changes his or her demeanor and the way they interact with neighbors. There is no living in the past if there is danger to other people or property based on these changes in behavior.

For residents who force you down this path: document, document. What and how to document accusations of any kind is a question for your attorney. Litigation based on false cause is costly and time consuming.

The possibility of lawsuits make many people tolerate actions that might be considered threatening. This is where inaction is an even more costly alternative - the blind eye mentality where known violent individuals are allowed to remain after their history is revealed.

As the first level of protection, perform a national background check on potential residents. Yes, this is more expensive than state only background checks, but people (and their problems) do cross state lines.

Suggest telling people who are confronted in some way, if at all possible, to first remove themselves from the area and immediately call authorities. As with smoke, a potential gas leak or fire do not hesitate to call 911. This is everyone's right in our society and the first line of defense against personal attacks.

It is difficult to have a blanket policy on "intimidation" or related actions. Municipalities have various moving parts on how to address this. Just know that ignoring this or similar acts is the worst possible solution. Be proactive, with counsel, in protecting the people and assets within your control.

# Swimsuit Edition (Pool Rules)

As summer approaches, commercial pools across the country welcome residents and friends of residents. Are your "pool rules" posted? No glass, no running. Postings about attire? We are generally unconcerned about attire. However, regarding what is tasteful, there is always someone willing to test the boundaries of public opinion.

Since most properties are without full time "pool police" good behavior is based substantially on the honor system. This honor system assumes (assume being one of my least favorite words) people will be guided by society's rules of decency. Are we fooling ourselves here? Decency, after all, is subjective.

For example: everyone likes a good looking swimsuit. We like them even more when displayed by someone who can wear them well. When it comes to clothing we hope common sense prevails. Whether in the bible belt or a stone's throw from Hollywood Blvd, we hope the "essentials" are covered and remain that way in our public areas on property.

Fortunately, at the property level, no one need be in charge of regulating good taste in swimwear. Unfortunately, there are those occasional lost souls (or drunken, or exhibitionist souls) who see the pool party audience as an opportunity to strut their stuff (literally). Here is where "community action" comes in.

Whereas many properties have on–site management, many do not. And those with a pool (an unsupervised pool) must rely on self–patrolling of errant behavior.

Consider posting the office telephone number in the pool area so any residence or guest enjoying the pool can reach for their handy cell phone to report behavior that  endangers safety or quiet enjoyment.

Consider posting more rules than fewer rules. "No diving" cannot be presumed. Same with smoking. Unless it's posted as a non–smoking area then smoking is assumed to be allowed.

**Make absolutely certain to post pool hours.**

Check your pool insurance rider. It may have certain added pool postings that are required for your policy to remain in full force.

**Water, pool guests and animals are always a bad idea.**

Most municipalities have a minimum sign size. Find out prior to buying a new sign (that is three inches too small).

Pools are a seasonal community amenity that provide enjoyment and require responsible use. Pools are a leasing selling point and common area expense. Balancing practical use with enforcement of pool rules is an ongoing part of being in property management.

# Master Keys (My Precious)

Ever lost a master key? Ever had that floor–dropping–from–under–you feeling while sitting in a chair on the phone? Master keys are necessary, they are also, truly, the keys to the kingdom of any property. Losing a single master key costs time and money. Immediate action is required. The exposure can be tremendous.

First and foremost, anyone in possession of a master key must be made fully aware of its significance. This responsibility is not to be taken lightly. Is there a "Smeagol" in your ranks? I have questions:

- How many master keys do you have out?
- Where are they– each and every one?
- Does each key have "Do Not Duplicate" stamped in it?
- Is there a plan in place for loss of a master key?
- Do you think electronic keys will be easier to manage on property?
- How long until you will be using keyless locks?

A few years ago my parents purchased a small Midwestern farm house. At closing the new owners were informed that in the last thirty years the doors were never locked, therefore, they had no keys. Did I mention this was a country house? There are many a hundred year–old house in Europe with keys just as old. For most of us, we have keys from manufacturers like Diebold, MasterLock, Schlage, Weslock, Yale, Weiser Locks, Sentry and American Lock.

Fission technology may replace gasoline as our primary power source in the future. But when? Like gasoline-based products in use for transportation, we may still be using brass keys twenty–five years from now, but they will represent the minority. Technological advances in locking "systems" are becoming less expensive and easier to install.

Earlier this summer I had cause to have an overnight stay in a town of less than five thousand people. There was one motel in town. It was a thirty year–old property with new electronic card key locks. Today most of us have a single key that opens all locks on property. Most of us are now, and into the foreseeable future stuck using fourteenth century technology– a real master key. Ugh. Ok. Let's get over the shock and try to make some progress here.

Silicon Valley is working on your future keys today. Future keys, or entry systems, will have components that include voice recognition, eye or fingerprint scans. Consider that in the future a small set of servers will process and maintain perhaps a billion "keys."

You will have keys that unlock doors and open windows based on pre–programming or "presence" (read facial recognition) similar to how motion lights work today, but with military technology upgrades a thousand times smarter than your current smart phone.

Professor Gary Shilling was recently asked about changes to commodities prices and their impact on the greater economy. He stated: "Price changes in commodities are cyclical. A poor crop is almost always followed by a good crop. But remember, just one hundred years ago nearly fifty percent of the population was engaged in agriculture, now it's less than one percent."

Locking systems are in transition. The futurist Michio Kaku was asked in a recent interview if all this "futurist stuff" was really possible. His response was: "one hundred years ago rapid transit was when your wagon was not stuck in the mud and mass communication was yelling out a window" (American Way June 2012).

Ask yourself, before Google, how did you find a plumber? I think fifty–years from now your Locksmith will have a degree in computer intelligence and a masters in Security Systems. Until then, be artfully careful with "my precious" with the underlying responsibility to "first do no harm."

# Leaving Things Broken

Property management is...bringing order to chaos with structured methodology.

How do you know when to leave broken things...broken? As seldom as possible, of course. Matters of public safety require immediate attention; water leaks, controlling utility costs, these are always near the top of the list.

## Dollars and Sense

Unfortunately, dollars and sense (spelled this way on purpose) requires you perform constant triage; giving the most attention to the areas that produce revenue or control expenditures. This "methodology" means some things do not get done.

Have you ever had to walk by the same exterior wall, time after time, knowing it needs painting (just one wall– not the whole building)? How hard can it be to paint a single wall??? Well let's see. First we must assess the wall for structural soundness, do any prep work necessary, probably apply primer or some type of sealant, then paint. There. Done.

## Prioritizing the Work

You already know the issue is not getting the wall painted; the issue is prioritizing the work. And in terms of running day–to–day operations from make–readys to electrical problems or addressing water leaks, painting an ugly wall is low on the list. Prioritize the work and have responsibility centers. Then there is always the matter of items that jump the line. So how do you get to that "one wall?"

Initially by making sure non-essential work stays on the list no matter how long the list. The wall in need of paint stays on the list even if at the very bottom, for a long time. Who wants to replace gutters? Anyone? Want to and need to are two different things, of course. So want to or not eventually there will be gutters that require replacing...make sure this stays on the to–do list.

**What's Broken?**

Sometimes what's "broken" is ownership. Property management cannot usually fix broken ownership, but you are there to guide their hand to the best of your ability. Maybe a re–fi is in order to free up capital expenditure dollars. Maybe there is an improved method for addressing vendor relationships that has an up front sunk cost but will pay for itself three times over. These are examples of potential owner assist that management can bring to owners.

Sometimes what's "broken" is management. Ownership must determine the factors that lead to considering a management change. Not all markets are good markets. You may have a stellar management team doing the absolute best they can considering market dynamics. What ownership should not do is "auto–default" into assuming that problematic operations are exclusively the result of management. Communication is key to ascertaining problematic areas. Once determined, problem solving can begin.

You never want to leave broken things broken but at the same time you must live within budget. This requires prioritizing tasks that maintain stabilized operations.

# Property Management Triage at Full Tilt

In property management "stuff happens." Being in emergency mode all the time is an unsustainable posture. And while emergencies happen... that's no reason to be caught off guard. There is just no physical method to run at full tilt all the time without losing focus and having productivity drop off. Preparedness gives us that breathing room to respond at a pace commensurate with the issue.

As an example, consider there are many manufacturing plants with three shifts; daytime, swing shift (4PM to Midnight) and graveyard (11PM to 7AM). A closer look will reveal different output targets for each. Generally, the people on day shift have higher output quotas than crews working other shifts. These output quotas follow the rule of diminishing returns that tells us marginal output may increase, but not at the same rate as optimum performance.

We have the medical field to thank for triage; a method of prioritizing work. Triage is used to sort medical cases in order of priority based on need in life and death situations. Here are a few things you can do in property management that follow triage–like methodologies.

**Use Triage**. The first order of business in an emergency situation is to use triage. The first question to answer is who is in charge of triage? Does everyone know the chain of command in an emergency? Is the plan of action accessible to this point person? Do they know what to do first?

**Preparedness**. No one can prepare for every emergency, for every potential occurrence, but we can have a plan of action. A simple example is making sure to have after–hours telephone numbers for plumbing. As we know, stuff happens. Many multifamily properties have units with only one bathroom per unit. An overflowing toilet with a broken shut off valve at midnight is a costly repair but far less costly than letting water run until morning.

**Bring in a specialist**.   Some emergencies are immediate, other emergencies allow us time to think and react. Assuming there is thinking time, bring in the specialist early in the situation. It could be something as simple as drywall behind a water damage repair where the emergency was repaired immediately. Don't linger in getting the drywall done and, if need be, bring in a specialist (outside contractor) to complete the work.

The emergency could be a downed tree. Although the tree may have created no harm, try not to make excuses for leaving it on the ground for a week or a month. Bring in a specialist to get it gone. The objective here is to remove any future hazard from exposed pipes, or tree limbs, etc. Include clean up as the last phase of the emergency and finish the job.

Triage assumes a plan of action for implementation. Do you have a plan? Does everyone know who the point person is for this plan? Past the initial phase of emergency response, call on the specialist necessary to knock out any remaining punch list.  Remove a one day emergency on property from being an ongoing source of management time and related resources.

# 10 Ways to Measure Your Success

Have you set the professional bar for your property management team? Do they know when they have hit the mark? Are responsibility centers clear? Let's discuss some measures that let you identify positive progress with a multifamily asset. Following is a short list of high value areas to commit "thinking time." We are applying these benchmarks to stabilized assets.

1. **The "So what" question?** Every PhD student knows about the "so what" question. Having spent months and perhaps years on a very succinct research question, a committee member says to the student "so what?" The follow up question being, "Why is this relevant?" Keep the "so what" question in mind as you work through this list. If your answers make you feel warm and fuzzy and look good on paper but have no functional use, so what?

2. **Occupancy.** Is your occupancy at or higher than competitive assets in your submarkets? View the broader submarket and market for intelligence. It is important to know where competitors are, operationally, to assist in measuring where to place your resources (dollars and manpower).

    Concessions and marketing seem to work in cycles. Sometimes price is all important, other times a free $100 fuel card kicks over leasing activity. Knowing what competitors are doing (that's working) on a real time basis is important to know.

3. **Collections.** Where are you on collections on the first, fifth and tenth of the month? Are systems in place and in use that positively affect collections outcomes?

4. **Resident retention.** Is your management team ahead of the curve on renewals; 45, 60 or 90 days ahead of lease end dates? Planning ahead makes for stabilized operations.

5. **Controlling expenses**. Are you comparing service providers for competitiveness? Do you know line item cost as compared to recent quarters and year–over–year?

6. **Response to maintenance.** Are you delivering a consistent product to customers? Have you set up reasonable expectations with customers and do you meet or exceed those expectations?

7. **Personnel turnover.** Do you know where your people are...in terms of their commitment to property management and being in your employ?

8. **Market presence.** Do you know your standing in the marketplace? Have you reviewed apartment review sites to see what people are saying about your assets? Can you answer this question: "What is your asset known for?" Is this positive or negative? If positive, how can you promote this aspect? If negative, how can you diminish the impact of this information or turn around the reputational harm?

9. **Owner Reports.** Are they consistent and informative? Are they concise?

10. **Do you maintain a vision?** This requires thinking time. Do you have time to think?

Back to #1. Were your responses useful to your organization, to the assets in your care? We began with a few questions. Have you set the professional bar for your property management team? Do they know when they have hit the mark? Are responsibility centers clear? We end this article with the question, "Do you maintain vision?" Lots of questions. Take on one at a time.

# Property Management Passion Fruit

Is it true that to be a good property manager you have to be a little like passion fruit; hard on the outside and soft and sweet on the inside? Property management (PM) is hard work. And while "Five Hour Energy" drinks are all well and good, who wants to drink two a day every day?

Are you a gerbils on that never–ending wheel? Granted, there are properties with full time staff devoted to sweeping common areas every day. Reality is many PM's are picking up in the parking lot from the time they get out of their car until reaching the office door. So how do you keep the passion and not burn out? Here are a few ideas.

**Prioritizing work.** Everything cannot be a priority. Honest. I've tried it. It's like dropping jello from a tall building and expecting it to land in a square pattern– to my understanding this has yet to occur. Prioritizing means you have to choose / select / decide.

**Create and/or implement Responsibility Centers.** Guess what? If you are a full blown professional property manager and you die tomorrow there will be someone there the next day to take your place. Sorry for being so blunt but it's true. The frame here isn't to say "so why kill yourself at work", the frame is to be productive and utilize the tools / people / resources at your disposal.

The only thing worse than having under–utilized responsibility centers is having them and not using them. They are there for a reason, hopefully manned. Have you ever flown a kite on a ten foot string? Ineffective, right? In fact, the more space between you and the kite, to a point, allows for better control of flight. PM is very similar in that you have to trust your people to do their jobs. Micro– managing has no place in running stabilized assets. Let the string out...

**Rest/Recharge. Disconnect.** Yes, we are oh so important. I recently watched a real estate related show on CNN where the broker claimed to have nine blackberry's. Nine? So while you are important to and within your business there becomes a point of diminishing returns if, say, every day after 2:00 is nap time to accommodate burnout. Another sign that rest is in order is when every sentence starts with "um."

I will admit this is a somewhat selfish missive as I too struggle in each of the aforementioned categories. Perfect time to state the obvious; do what I say and not what I do... I am reminding myself, and you, that balancing work and non–work is absolutely necessary to give your best in both venues. There is always room for improvement. The key is to avoid "constant crazy" in the race that will in fact continue past the span of our careers. How? Prioritize, implement responsibility centers, rest/recharge.

When you love what you do it's easy to be passionate about it. Maintaining our passion requires working smart. Maintaining our passion requires trusting our people, getting rest and working on the right priorities. Sounds like a plan to me. Where's that kite string?

# Websites for Improving Your PM Team

As busy property management professionals we only have so much time for industry–related activities. Yet keeping current, staying relevant in our selected field of expertise, is part of staying ahead of the curve. The choices can be over–whelming. Do we devote our training dollars to in–house activities and become actively engaged in local and regional associations or national events?

Following are five websites that can engage your property management team and keep them on the top of their game. None require travel outside of your marketplace to garner benefits (of course, you may decide on some travel for national events) .

**Multifamily Executive**. MFE is like my personal multifamily "USA Today" on the industry. There is a lot of material, it's concise and provides a starting point for further inquiry.

**Lumosity.** This site is more than "mind games." Lumosity provides learning exercises for your brain that can focus your attention at work and away.

**Multifamilybiz.com**. The most comprehensive list of upcoming multifamily related conferences. There is just no way to send everyone to every industry related conference. Use this website to see what's coming up nationally and regionally. This will provide you with a planning horizon to pick and choose which conferences will most benefit your team.

**REIT's**. A website by the National Association of Real Estate Investment Trusts. A REIT is a Real Estate Investment Trust. REIT's are some of the biggest owners of multifamily in the country. Identify the largest multifamily REIT's in your marketplace and follow their activity. Are they net buyers or sellers in your market? Do they self–manage or hire third–party managers? How many people do they employ in your market? Who are their preferred vendors? Identify those your firm is competing with and see what they are up to in your backyard.

**Marcus Millichap Brokerage.** You don't have to be in buy or sell mode to benefit from knowing about transactions in your marketplace. This brokerage company has offices nationwide focused on multifamily. For your PM team, their website has stellar research on national and regional trends. From my perspective, their research is some of the best in the business related to multifamily. (Multifamily Insight has no affiliation with this company.)

# Chapter 3

## Demographics and Market Analysis

# Multifamily & Educational Attainment

It is well documented that third–grade reading levels tell us much about adult achievement. There is a direct correlation between personal income and educational attainment. Overstating the obvious, people with a college degree make more money than those dropping out of high school.

Do investors select multifamily assets to acquire based on local school achievement tests? How about buying multifamily based on educational attainment of the individuals residing in submarkets? The latter offers a better correlation of future value.

Three cities in the United States with some of the lowest high school graduations rates are Detroit, Las Vegas and Miami. Does that mean these cities are unattractive markets for investment? The answer cannot be established based exclusively on high school graduation rates. The reason being that a high percentage of people residing in these cities migrated there from somewhere else. Why? Jobs. People follow jobs.

While it's important to factor in reading level, educational attainment and high school graduation rates in the local soup (I mean in the demographic review of a place) it is more important to identify the educational attainment of current residents.

Picking on my home state, the school districts for the two largest cities in the state are both on the verge of being unaccredited. This slows potential investment. The manufacturing industry has a very high interest in the reading/writing skill levels generated from local schools. This is where they draw their workers from– for generations.

Multifamily assets are seldom viewed like manufacturing plants. A multifamily property manager is looking for residents with the ability to pay market rents and the desire to sign a one–year lease. A manufacturer is seeking tax abatement and a place to grow roots for multiple years.

The manufacturer needs to be certain that the local populous can deliver on necessary skills to man the plant. Both businesses need people; the manufacturing business needs people who can provide a certain minimum competency, the multifamily business needs people who can afford market rents.

Part of determining the future value of a multifamily asset is the willingness of businesses to invest in the community. Once this dissipates there is seldom anything a multifamily owner/manager can do. Business support is much deeper than just retail. Look at historic occupancy of industrial and office space. This can be an indicator of job in–flows/out–flows. Review average household income, median income and per capita income.

Changes in investment via the local chamber of commerce, through the Bureau of Labor Statistics and various paid services providing real time changes and patterns in job growth, income growth, household formation and retail sales. It is important to review these numbers for the metro area, surrounding submarkets and the submarket in question. Include a review of traffic counts, current and historic.

Reading levels delivered to the community by a local school district is a single touchstone in the review process of a market and its asset. But it can turn into the eye of the storm when it comes to a review of overall business investment in a place. Discount this metric at your own risk. Reading levels and educational attainment are necessary components in your review funnel of demographic analysis when performing acquisitions due diligence.

# Construction Starts and Household Formation

I can tell you with a high degree of certainty that as household formation picks up steam multifamily construction is well below future demand. Here is a definition of household formation from a report issued by housingamerica.org entitled, "What Happens to Household Formation in a Recession?" by Gary Painter of University of Southern California.

*"New households can be formed either when children move out of their parents' homes, when couples separate or when unrelated individuals choose to live singly after previously sharing a residence."*

Household formation drives demand in multifamily construction. As household formation accumulate to measurable numbers we will also see increasing construction starts. And this time, with a much sharper pencil and focus on urban markets. There will be limited tertiary construction with a hope and prayer that "they will come."

As job creation returns, more adults leave living arrangements with family members necessitated by recessionary pressures. This increase in household formation will place added pressure on multifamily demand. As the rate of household formation increases, concurrent with years of low multifamily construction starts, vacancy will decrease and rent growth will escalate.

An ongoing misnomer is that "shadow inventory" is dampening demand for apartment rentals. Not true. Of the ten million single–family homes representing this supposed shadow inventory six million are in various stages of foreclosure. Translation = unavailable for rental.

Foreclosures eventually clear. Regardless, housing construction starts (single–family and multifamily) remain well below future demand.

U.S. Census Bureau staff released a paper in early 2011 entitled, **"The Effects of Recession on Household Composition: "Doubling Up" and Economic Well–Being,"** by Laryssa Mykyta and Suzanne Macartney, U.S. Census Bureau. They reference Mr. Painter's definition and add Census statistics. From the article:

"One way people may cope with challenging economic circumstances is to combine households and household resources with other families or individuals."

The abstract states, in part, that those most likely to double up were adults not in the workforce. Conclusion: As availability of jobs increases, doubling up reverses.

Population keeps increasing, albeit at a drip pace, but still increasing. And with recent job creation ticking up, Junior and his bride–to–be are finding opportunities to move from the nest and form their own household. Mom is happy. Junior is happy. Bride is real happy.

We will see more construction occur within close-in suburbs, new single–family and multifamily housing attached at the fencepost to rail, light rail and rapid transit systems. As Professor Shiller is apt to say, "x–urbs" may well be behind us.

Jobs are key and jobs are first created in urban areas where synergies exists. Waiters and welders both work in cities in urban environments- and expand from these dense places to suburbs, x–urbs and beyond. Our densely populated cities will become denser with people tepidly leaving the "safety in numbers" for suburban environs.

If you wonder about how the gainfully employed feel about leaving a finally found job, ask anyone unemployed for twelve or more consecutive months. I submit that their commute is shorter than ever before as they identify housing within a stone's throw of their job. Yes, increases in household formation will create demand for multifamily– but close to job centers first and foremost.

# Five Reasons Why Occupancy is Sky High

Occupancy is high for the same reason gasoline goes up right before Labor Day: Supply and demand. There are a few other reasons, of course. Let's explore them.

**1. Mortgage squeeze.** How many people do you know who have applied for mortgage financing? How many obtained the loan? As if refinancing were not difficult enough, new rules imposed by Fannie/Freddie have increased the standards banks must meet to sell their originated loans to a GSE (Government Sponsored Entity).

While banks have the option of keeping a mortgage in house, standard operating procedure is to sell off each loan to the GSE's so those mortgage funds can be loaned again. Alas, if a loan does not meet the requisites for an immediate sale then most lenders will decline the loan. Fewer loans, more renters...

**2. Lower home ownership rate.** Fewer home loans means fewer home owners. There are $5M fewer families who own their own home today as compared to 2008. Fewer home owners, more renters...

**3. Low wages for new wage earners.** Wages remain stagnant. For new college graduates, those in highly sought after fields are finding plenty of options. But for others requiring immediate "re–training" the road to stable employment is longer. When wages remain flat people are less inclined to feel good about their future, i.e., less likely to make big commitments– like buying a house. Not only are loans hard to come by, but if a family's earned income is lower than five years ago this tends to dampen future expectations. Low wages, low wage expectations equals more renters...

**4. Five years of "below trend" construction starts.** New construction housing starts have hovered around 600,000 each year for several years. Just to keep pace with nominal population growth and make up for homes (and apartments) that are removed from inventory, we need over 1,000,000 new homes built each year. Multiply this construction shortfall by five years and the gap begins to become obvious. Fewer new homes available for sale, more renters...

**5. Decrease in existing housing inventory**. With limited new housing product coming on line and foreclosure activity slowing the inventory is... not much. Many market's are seeing the swing from a buyer's market to a seller's market. The cause is limited additions to supply, less mobility and families staying in their home longer. Fewer existing homes available for sale, more renters...

The real estate cycle seldom stays in balance for long. We are in a constant state of flux from oversupply to absorption to equilibrium and expansion. Seems that equilibrium is always the shortest of cycles. I believe the pending housing shortage cycle will be longer than most people imagine. It just takes too much time to get new product to market.

Consider also that construction financing, while not a thing of the past, removes from consideration any but the most well heeled developers. Thus, over–shooting demand, this time, will be difficult to achieve as small developers are left on the sidelines without financing.

We may not see double digit rent growth (other than in 24–hour cities) but 3%+ or greater will be the national norm for the next several years with consistently high occupancy.

# Multifamily Apartments: Five Big Trends

What "big trends" are driving the multifamily industry? It's easy to get lost in the minutia of multifamily. Following are five trends occurring in multifamily that will take up more space in your email box and brain in coming years.

1. **Technology**. Rapid technological advances cannot to be ignored. It's imperative to be a "first adopter" in an attempt to keep pace. When a twelve year old can help Mommy find an apartment on their smart phone we need to be there; on mobile, online, with current information and availability.

Tech is part of your daily life on every level from the food you eat to the units you lease. Technology allows you to connect with your customers broadly and specifically. From Living Social to Facebook to PayPal there is no getting around greater forthcoming technology integration in multifamily. Carve out your niche here and own it. Note that this cannot be 100% outsourced. Someone in house must know where all the wires are located.

2. **Decrease in family size**. From 2000 to 2010 average family size has decreased by about one percent. Many would say this is statistically insignificant. But let's translate that number into the increase in households created.

According to *America's Families and Living Arrangements: 2010*, the average household size declined to 2.59 in 2010, from 2.62 people in 2000. This is partly because of the increase in one–person households, which rose from 25 percent in 2000 to 27 percent in 2010, more than double the percentage from 1960 (13 percent). These data come from the 2010 Current Population Survey, that provides a look at the socioeconomic characteristics of families and households at the national level.

In 2010 there were approximately 114 million households in the U.S. Therefore, a one percent increase in the number of homes needed (to house the same number of people, but with fewer people per household) equates to a need for an additional 1.1 million homes. Conclusion: smaller household size equates to increases in household formation.

3. **Decrease in unit size**. SRO (Single Resident Occupancy) and Micro Units are a trend that will only expand. Construction of Micro's provides a completely different perspective on unit count, density and livability. It's a positive when considering transportation districts that allow for greater utilization of existing infrastructure.

Few people think about how much architects affect our daily lives. They keep us safe with progressive street level designs and keep us healthy with recognition that humans need sunlight. While multifamily developers require continuous value engineering, architects want to deliver livable space. Now they will be asked to do this with smaller and smaller individual unit footprints. Think of a stack unit washer/dryer where in the future the same single machine will wash and dry while taking up half the space.

4. **Increases in urbanization.** Jobs are in the cities– jobs and job growth reside most fully in the urban core. Proximity to jobs and cultural events are in the cities. Suburbia is great if you can afford it, but usually requires individual access to transportation. Anticipate continued increases in fuel, insurance and commute times. This is the trade off in pure financial terms; live closer to work and pay more in rent or live further from work and pay more for transportation (including personal time based on commuting distance).

5. **Multifamily product scarcity (demand).** Everyone knows that multifamily construction starts have increased. Will this be enough to meet pending residential demand? Considering Item #2 above, the answer is no. Consider also that in recent years construction starts were well below delivering just replacement housing (construction of units to "replace" those lost to age, natural disaster and redevelopment).

Add population increases and fewer people per household to this equation and a gap begins to develop; low construction starts, plus smaller household size, plus population gains equates to demand exceeding supply.

Recap. Stay current on technology. Recognize that unit sizes are getting smaller, and that more people are moving back to the urban core, be aware of decreasing average household size. Stay in tune with your local market to take advantage of your soon–to–be scarce product type. And do all these things at the same time. Just another day at the office, right?

# Clinical Definition of a Submarket

Submarkets are boundaries that define where a property competes. Having specialized knowledge at the submarket level is a significant strategic advantage over your competitors. A submarket it:

- An area with similar properties in terms of physical stock and rents
- An area that reflects patterns of locational preference
- Represented by transportation patterns, natural barriers
- Inclusive of competitive properties
- Snapshot of resident demographics and workforce metrics

A submarket will seldom be a perfect radius or a square box. Depending on geography, the market area can be a serpentine impression or L–shaped figure. Define the geographic area of your submarkets using the bullet points above.

Some things we know to our core, right? The effect of vacancy on revenue; that crime in a neighborhood will eventually impact the reputation of your assets; that a bad mortgage loan will be front and center at the absolute worst time in the business cycle. Many of these things can be avoided through proactive management.

How far ahead of the curve are you with respect to the changing demographics surrounding your assets? It's easy to be complacent. We think "we know what we know." You live, work, eat and sleep, usually, within close proximity to the assets owned or managed. Surely, will be the first to know about plant closings, an influx of immigrants, a "brain drain" from local institutions.

How? How will you know these things? And how will you react to such knowledge? More importantly, how will this knowledge impact your decision–making at the property level? Will you take advantage of these "signals?" They can tell you when to sell, when to double down your investment; when to change marketing strategies to scoop up new residents everyone else is ignoring.

Submarkets are the boundaries that define where a property must compete and where property comparisons begin. In a study using 50 metropolitan–area markets:…between 40% and 50% of a property's overall performance is explained by sub–market factors while only 10% is explained by metropolitan factors (Submarkets Matter! Applying Market Information to Asset–Specific Decisions– Real Estate Finance Fall 2000).

This is not a grow or die strategy. More likely, it is a know or die strategy from lack of paying attention. The assets in your care are very important. If you don't care about the demographic changes surrounding them, who will?

# Beating the Averages

While no one wants to be average, researchers often get stuck devoting a lot of time to ascertaining "average" household income, "average job growth, "average" drive times. Do you really care if the outputs of demographic research represents the mean, median or mode? Probably not. What is it we really need to know? Trends... we need to know the trends.

In 2013, multifamily developers delivered approximately 160,000 new multifamily units into the marketplace. In 2014, this number rose to over 350,000. Now that's a trend worth noting, particularly if one, three or five percent of this total is coming into your marketplace.

When it comes to changes in population and income, focus on the market or trade area most affecting your assets: Focus on the submarket. Extended research has proven that almost 50% of future yield is determined by submarket trends. So while it is nice to know the direction of trends occurring in Chicago, if your assets are in Schaumburg (overstating the obvious) then focus on Schaumburg.

**Submarkets represent the area where a property must compete**

A submarket includes the subject property and the geographic area encompassing directly competitive properties. An extended definition includes the geographic area encompassing directly competitive properties and the area where most existing residents commute for jobs– not just for your property, but for all properties in the submarket.

The shape of the submarket will seldom be round or square. Make sure to note natural and man–made barriers such as freeways or one–way streets that funnel traffic in a certain way either toward or away from the submarket.

## How to avoid being "average"

The way to avoid average numbers is to focus on annual percentage change at the submarket level. If creating your very own submarket is a struggle, then utilize block group and census tract data to get the ball rolling. And while is it all very nice to have everything drawn up on a computer generated map, swallow your pride and buy a paper map to begin the process and mark it up!

## Knowing the direction of change

There are two consistently overlooked areas in market demographics research in multifamily; one is knowing what we have, the second is knowing the direction of change. A BIG part of what we have and/ or what we are buying with an investment in a multifamily asset is an investment into an area that represents a certain demographic profile. Ignoring this is like flying blind: You can do it for a minute but the long–term effects are disastrous.

The remedy to flying blind (demographically speaking) is to perform an analysis of the in–place population looking at population trends that includes the number of people, their household income and average family size (this is a starter list but one that has easy to find data). Year–over–year, which way are the numbers going? How many years can you accurately determine? Can you create a trend, or projection, going forward from your findings? Doing so will place you miles ahead when making investment decisions.

# Five Free Mapping Resources

It's no small task to add a demographic component to your knowledge base about a particular property or portfolio. Getting "granular" by creating layered demographic maps can be very expensive. The more detail requested the more expensive the mapping outputs.

Broad mapping outputs are generally free. County and city maps, for example, provided by the U.S. Census Bureau are free and can generate an accurate guide on income, population and household information at the census tract level. But what if you want bus routes, or crime statistics? How about utilities availability or information on pending building permits or road construction?

The good news is that there are free resources that provide this information. The bad news is that the sources are "all over the map." Following are some places to start the search. Just remember, the more specific your search, the more time and/or money required to obtain the information.

**ESRI "Make a Map."** This company is the "big dog" on campus in the world of GIS (Geographic information Systems). This link takes to you to their "create a map" or make–a–map web page. Just plug in a city and state to gain access to census tract level data. You have to uncheck "Hide U.S. demographics" for the demographics to be visible. It's a mapping nerd thing, I think.

**ArcGIS Online**. This online resource has over 100,000 users creating maps for public and private consumption. Cities around the country are using this platform to generate public map galleries. One great example is the City of Salem Oregon (www.maps.cityofsalem. net). You have to download Microsoft Searchlight to use this resource. I think you will find useful and interesting maps specific to your marketplace.

**U.S Geological Survey (USGS).** You want aerial photos? How about satellite images? How about information on hazard areas and earthquake and flood zones? Here is the place to start...

**Neighborhood Scout.** Neighborhood Scout is all about crime stats at the local level. For crime statistics you would think that the best source is the Federal Bureau of Investigation. This is probably true for law enforcement professionals, but for the general public there is basically lots and lots of tables of aggregated data and no interactive maps. It's not the easiest site to navigate but it delivers crime outputs at the local level. As a test I selected Conyers Georgia with a population of 15,000 persons. This site broke down the city into ten components.

**Free Maps for Teachers** This site from Richard Byrne provides 21 mapping sites that teachers (and non–teachers) can use to create maps of all kinds; from Google Maps and Google Earth to maps that allow you to measure trips and create animation. Many of the sites allow you (the user) to create custom maps of your own.

# Demographics and Census 2020

Will we have a census in 2020? As government looks for places to cut expenditures the Census is ripe for slicing as there is no strong advocate within government to champion the cause. A recent article in the Washington Post suggests that Census 2020 will be performed electronically via the internet.

The census is invaluable to business and government. We redraw political boundaries based on census data, we can see population trend lines of growth and contraction. We obtain a very accurate gauge of where aging populations reside and where youth are congregating. All of these bits of information assist businesses, from retailers to home builders, in their decision–making.

The census is more than just a target marketing tool. Companies utilize census data regularly to assess workforce statistics. For example, a company looking to locate a manufacturing plant that will employ 300 high skill employees will want to know which cities have these workers available now and into the future.

A company will review, among other things, census data to ascertain average age and educational attainment of the existing workforce and cross–reference this with Bureau of Labor Statistics data to identify the number of existing people in the workforce that meets or exceeds minimum experience criteria. This tells them the number of potential qualified employees in the workforce in a particular place they will have in their initial hiring pool of qualified candidates.

Multifamily and new home builders need to know the direction of populations. The same for small business owners. A person looking to open and run a group home or a few guys wanting to open a new sandwich shop are all interested in knowing who lives in a place and the direction of the numbers in terms of age, income and household size. These facts represent the baseline data for building further layers of demographic information about a place.

Accurate census data allows government to estimate future social security obligations and measure the number of potential people available to serve in the armed forces. Why does one grocery store have five different kinds of hot peppers and another one five miles away stock two hundred varieties of red wine? Demographics.

Let's hope that Census 2020 is in no way watered down from prior versions. We may in fact obtain better estimates based on electronic versions being sent to heads of households. Advances in demography and statistical query will also play a role. My vote is for full funding to do the job right. We all benefit.

# Local Market Knowledge

When reviewing real estate for purchase there are varying types of local market knowledge; knowledge of the physical asset, the property around the physical asset, knowledge about the market, the submarket and the people who live and work close by. How deep is your local market knowledge? The data can be segregated into four categories:

- The subject asset–the potential acquisition candidate.

- Assets adjacent to the site– those properties that share a lot line with the subject property.

- The submarket–an area represented by certain natural and competitive trade area boundaries.

- The market–generally represented by the city or metropolitan statistical area.

**The subject asset**. There are physical and financial dynamics to address during due diligence and then operational considerations post closing. Not one of these is any less important than any other part of the process.

**Adjacent assets**. What do you know about the assets surrounding the assets you own/manage or are looking at as a potential purchase? Do you know who owns the properties on either side, in front and behind? What do you know about the age, condition or occupancy of these assets? Would you know if they were for sale without having to wait on seeing a "for sale" sign out front? Knowing your neighbors by name and number is very important presuming you have an interest in acquiring adjacent property when it becomes available. Particularly if you want your neighbors to know you are a potential buyer.

Having names and telephone numbers can be important, however, the deeper question is really more about use and intended use of the property. For example, if neighboring properties as far as the eye can see are all single family homes there is a good chance they will remain so for an extended period of time. However, if there are varying uses occurring then zoning changes could potentially bring added competition.

**The submarket**. Once the submarket is assessed, a multifamily property owner or management company has a very solid view of the population, income and competitive properties affecting a given apartment asset. Seldom is this area square or round. Nor does the shape or size follow census tracts or block groups. The shapes, sizes and area covered varies immensely.

**A submarket is a geographic area defined by streets, natural barriers and the specific properties in which a property is in competition for customers.**

Making a determination about population growth and income, and aligning this information with the number of housing and multifamily housing units will provide guidance about future vacancy and rent growth. These factors have significant impact on value.

**The market.** Markets are distinguished by size and quality. A market is where a rental property must compete represented by established boundaries. A market represents a place and its surrounding infrastructure including physical, social and cultural places. A market represents a place where people work, worship and go to school. It is an aggregate location with a certain cohesiveness.

All of these local market matters add to your specialized knowledge about a particular property. Reliance on the "drive by" is no longer sufficient nor is talking with a few "locals" to get a feel for a place. The more you know the higher your comfort level in the buy decision.

# Counting Cars

Do you know average "car counts" passing by each of your assets every day? How about average speed of the vehicles as they pass by? Is your marketing message capturing these potential customers?

Too many non–institutional multifamily owners treat marketing as a necessary evil rather than a continual part of the business. They believe it is an aspect of the business that can be  switched on and switched off at will.  Having a market presence requires consistency in message delivery. One of the ways to do this is by having appropriate signage with the right message.

Multifamily remains a very fragmented marketplace. There are assets in places with 100,000 vehicles a day passing their front door, others with zero traffic: as in none.  I have visited properties that practically sit on top of freeways and others requiring four and five turns (or a round-about) into a small suburban subdivision just to see the entrance to the property.

Identifying car counts for your assets can be as simple as contacting the local planning and zoning office. P&Z is responsible for knowing the "load" for each street in the municipality.  The load factor allows for road expansion as necessary and scheduling road maintenance and repairs.

The old fashioned way of gaining car counts is to get out a lawn chair and small cooler.  Find a shady spot and "count cars" during peak times (morning and afternoon commute times).  It may sound silly but the information gained is invaluable to your marketing efforts.

For properties with good street visibility and high vehicle traffic designing appropriate signage requires knowing average vehicle speed.  Whereas presenting the name and telephone number of the property is best, at sixty miles an hour people are just as likely to capture your website address.  Leave off the "www" as this is no longer necessary. Removing "www" also gives you more space for the web address.

For assets with zero car traffic, where signage is important so that people know when they have arrived, marketing requires getting people to your site with the most direct route. Thus, every marketing piece should have "easy to find" directions even if the directions are somewhat involved. The objective is to reduce the barrier to entry, or in this case, to gaining showings.

Every multifamily asset is unique and so is its car count. Knowing car counts is imperative to gaining knowledge for implementing marketing best practices appropriate to the asset.

# Connecting Rent Growth to Job Growth

Are you looking for rent growth? Follow the jobs. It seems like such a simple concept. Remember that jobs are mobile too and the theory becomes a little more ethereal. Drilling down a layer or two brings to question; what type of jobs?

Historically the "big news items" related to jobs were about manufacturing jobs– a plant opening, a plant closing. Such an event brought instant price movement to nearby rental assets as people responded to news of the event. Today's marketplace is much more fluid and dispersed. Here's a technology related example. This year Yahoo and Hewlett–Packard have both announced that "work at home" is banned. Both companies have stated that while they are aware of potential productivity losses, they expect gains in collaborative synergies.

As of this writing, Yahoo employs approximately 12,000 people. More than one–third worked from home. That's over 4,000 families who may consider a change in housing based on the realities of having a daily commute. This represents a change in job mobility. Or does it? It's really a change in "housing mobility" as the jobs have not changed location. It's about housing mobility because a portion of this workforce may change their housing location now that a daily commute is involved.

In this example there is no change in the number of jobs, but a significant change in commuter patterns that will affect rent growth in those areas closest to Yahoo job centers. Consider how this one change in corporate policy will impact rent growth for certain assets!

The objective here is to spur your thinking with respect to the normalized big announcements about jobs recognizing also that announcements and reality often have lag time and a disparity between the announcement and actual occurrences.

Take for example the announcement that a company is bringing 300 jobs into an area. Further research may reveal that this will occur over three years. Check back in a year and the reality may be that only 50 jobs have actually materialized so far for a myriad of reasons.

Another bite at the apple requires us to look at full–time vs. part–time job creation. An announcement of 500 new "part–time" jobs in reality may represent only 200 FTE (Full Time Equivalent) jobs.

When you think about job growth look at the stability of the existing employment base first, then consider increases in job growth as a percentage of the existing employment base. This will bring some realism into your thinking regarding the potential impact of new positions and their effect on rent growth in the local market place.

# Chapter 4

## Multifamily Financing

# Finding Perfect Leverage

Perfect leverage means different things to different people. The best financial leverage to place on an asset is financing that promotes an alignment between the objectives of ownership and the financial needs of the asset.

Remember that property assets do not have feelings; but people do. Unfortunately, too many investors allow their "feelings" to affect financial decisions. I am a firm believer in bringing in high quality expertise into the mortgage financing decision. There is no reason for you to go this alone or settle for second-rate help. Hire, engage and seek out professional counsel.

This is not a conversation about yield or IRR. Under the presumption that an acquisition is for long-term hold then financing that matches this objective is concurrently in the best interest of the owners and that of the asset.

Financial leverage was a dirty word for a season. This is not to say people reverted to 100% cash deals. However, the pendulum has swung widely in recent years from commercial mortgages with an interest only component to those requiring 25% cash and a substantial balance sheet to get a meeting.

Think for a moment about real estate financing in Asia, particularly Japan and China. Japan is a democratic society with open and free capital markets; yet for the longest time residential real estate financing presumed a five-year amortization schedule. And that's it- no more.

China is a non-democratic society with highly regulated markets. China has more than thirty cities with populations greater than ten million people in each of these cities! Many are industrial job centers. The government decides what is built and where it is built. Think about applying for a mortgage in that environment! How does that make you feel?

The U.S. mortgage system has it quirks, certainly. However, the system is very well developed and very stable with well-known rules and regulations. (We exclude here references to the Fed, quantitative easing, changes in bank regulations, the meltdown of Lehman, Bank of America buying Countrywide, etc).

Finding the right commercial mortgage is the beginning step to applying appropriate leverage to an asset. Utilize the full extent of your network to identify professionals in the field to assist you in gaining access to the right money sources. There are no shortcuts here. It is very time-consuming, yes. However, if the reward is long-term financial stability the effort is a worthy pursuit.

# Banking, Energy and Real Estate (Circa 2050)

It's now the year 2050. History has a habit of repeating. People have short memories and all of our institutional knowledge does not transfer from one generation to the next. This is where the saying comes from that "Those who are unaware of history are bound to repeat it."

Based on a recent downturn in the world economy some of the largest banks in the world are reducing capital availability-even to their best customers. As we know from history and the "great recession" of 2008, when credit availability is reduced abruptly there can be a ripple effect throughout whole economies.

With only five "super banks" remaining the herd is small. Yet the herd mentality remains. With the collapse of Exxon, based on break–through fission technology rendering oil as practically useless, trillions of dollars in loans secured by oil related infrastructure is in jeopardy. Nations that rely on oil for the vast majority of Gross Domestic Product are cashing out of long–term investments to balance trade deficits. What is Nuclear Fission Technology?

*Nuclear fission energy is a competitive and mature low–carbon technology, operating to high levels of safety within the EU. Most of the current designs are Light Water Reactors (LWR), capable of providing base–load electricity often with availability factors of over 90%. http:// setis.ec.europa.eu/publications/technology–information–sheets/ nuclear–fission–technology–information–sheet*

*Nuclear fission is a process in nuclear physics in which the nucleus of an atom splits into two or more smaller nuclei as fission products, and usually some by–product particles. http://www.sciencedaily. com/articles/n/nuclear_fission.htm*

Earlier this century a move that seemed purely political is now prophetic. The Chancellor of Germany in 2013 announced all gold held by German banks and her government to domicile the metal in their country. With the oil infrastructure now worthless and gold nearing $10,000 an ounce the two super banks based in Germany are the strongest of the lot.

In times such as these hard assets have the greatest staying power: real estate, gold, quality collectibles. While inflation deteriorates the value of cash, hard assets have a better chance of keeping pace with inflation thereby maintaining their inflation–adjusted value.

Real estate assets are best held with little or no leverage to reduce exposure to high interest rates. But there is still risk. Thirty year mortgages written in 2025 with interest rate caps of 30% (seemingly impossible at the time) are now approaching those rates. Credit balances that were written at 12% are approaching 50% as banks determine how to weather the storm.

**Is this fiction?**

This post is intended to make you think past present day realities and plan beyond next quarter or next year. Things change. Sometimes abruptly. Some scientists believe fission energy will replace carbon based fuels in as little as fifty years. Concurrently, based on the nuclear accident in Japan, Germany shut down its nuclear power plants.

In the futuristic movie "I Robot" the character played by Will Smith buys a round of beers for two and the bill comes to $48.00. Is that fiction? Let's hope. But if not then remember that hard assets such as real estate usually keep pace with inflation over time. Land and buildings in densely populated urban areas will retain value. Farm land will retain value.

In this scenario the future cost of gasoline will be $20 a gallon or zero. Care to guess which one? Either way, consider owning real estate as part of your investment portfolio. Quality real estate.

# Multifamily Finance and Predatory Lending

Predator lenders will prey on anyone. Their field of expertise remains un–restrained. Why rip off five or ten consumers when one fake large commercial loan can yield the same output (for the predator).

The single best method for avoiding predatory lenders is to talk to lenders; lots and lots of lenders. The mortgage banking business is filled with hard working, honest, sincere professionals. The profession also has its fair share of sharks and stingrays. The only way to tell the difference is to network.

One method used by scam artists and predator lenders is to isolate their potential mark (that would be you) and smother the person with so much attention and paperwork they have no time or appetite to discuss the matter with outside parties. These "outside parties" (according to the predator lender) are people like your spouse, business partners, friends and other lenders.

Another method is when the predator attempts to place YOUR loan on THEIR timeline. Sounds reasonable at first as any loan must have a start and finish timeline. The issue with the predator lender that should raise suspicion is when their timeline has nothing whatsoever to do with your timeline.

For example, if the current mortgage has six months remaining until the first day it can be paid in full without penalty, a predator lender demanding loan fees and third party costs be paid NOW should raise suspicion, right? As in the normal course of business, appraisals cannot be completed months prior to closing a new loan. If they are this just increases your costs as the appraisal will require an update.

When it comes to obtaining a commercial loan the best thing is to STAY IN THE MAINSTREAM. The mainstream includes community banks (local), nationally known lending sources, members of the Mortgage Bankers Association and known insurance companies. Another way of saying this is to do business with people who can be found without much trouble.

One of my friends who has traveled the world shared with me that his best experiences were when he sought out certain people and places, vs. when people sought him out (as a known tourist) and being dragged to places he had little interest. I think the same holds true when seeking a commercial loan. If you are being dragged into the loan, let go of the rope. Better to fall where you are than suffer more damage.

Being in the real estate business on a full time basis means you already know some lenders. If those you know are unable to assist with the type or amount of loan you seek, ask for referrals. Being a known entity in the business, people you know will assist in this endeavor.

If you're not on LinkedIn® by now PLEASE join. This is a great place to network. Add me as a contact; I welcome connect invites. Join Property Management Professionals on LinkedIn®; this is the biggest PM group on LinkedIn®. Also, check out Multifamily Biz. This site is a great resource for conferences and real time news in the industry including who is getting loans done.

When in need of a commercial loan, start with people you know, go next to referrals and then local and national resources where the people working there can be contacted in the normal course of business. Avoid people you can never meet (even if you wanted to) or those working exclusively from a cell phone and those with no street address.

My objective here is not to shut out the independent broker–lender. But too many times I've talked to people who shipped off a two–page "loan application" with a $10,000 cashiers check that was never seen again. Don't let this be you.

# Paperwork with a Purpose

For those engaged in financing a multifamily asset, the task of gathering loan documentation or paperwork can range from days to months. You can complain the whole way through but this just seems to make the process take even longer.

Stressing over the paperwork is like drinking coffee at midnight when you thought it was decaf–this is not helpful. One strategy I use to shorten the process is preparedness. Pre–submission preparedness.

What makes for a viable loan process? First and foremost, a timeline. Knowing the anticipated timeline prior to applying allows for some mental preparation for the road ahead. Add to this a lender-provided "checklist" and you can visualize yourself in the starting blocks for the run ahead.

The starting gun fires with delivery of the credit application to your loan officer or commercial mortgage broker. We can presume there were some general meetings of the mind at this point; enough that you have determined this is the right course of action. That said, the best thing that you can do is not fight them with respect to getting your paperwork in. Protracted loan application processing is often caused by the borrower.

This is a team effort. Removing the "them vs. us" perspective is one of the most helpful things to accomplishing the tasks at hand. Hey, if you don't want the money, don't apply for the loan. If you do want the money, do the work–the paperwork.

When the borrower causes the loan process to slow it usually has to do with a lack of organization with respect to providing required documentation; tax returns, financials or entity information that should be readily available. This is counter–productive, of course, as we presume the borrower is applying for a loan because, um, they want a loan. What's the remedy?

Collect most of the lender's "checklist" information prior to submitting the loan application or credit release form.

Once the lender is selected and you have their checklist, get to work. When the majority of the information is in your possession THEN sign and send the credit application followed by the requested documentation.

There will always be straggler documents, things you are waiting on from someone else. By requesting these docs prior to submitting your credit app you can truthfully state they were requested and that they are "in process." The commercial loan process may seem like a high mountain (of paperwork) but like anything else one step at a time gets you closer to accomplishing the tasks.

Complaining about the paperwork gets you no closer to loan closing. Providing the paperwork as required by the lender does drive the loan towards closing.

Break down the checklist into individual doable pieces. Ask lots of questions, ask for explanations about anything that is not crystal clear in your mind. Stay on pace. As closing day approaches you will have less and less to do. The checklist will be completely "checked"– because you've already done it!

Throughout history people have attempted to buy/sell/finance assets that do not belong to them. Today's world is no different. The documentation required to complete a loan is all necessary in the eyes of the lender. The bottom line is that no money will change hands without proof of title, proof of signing authority, proof of good title. Paperwork, paperwork...

# The Seller Carry–back (Seller Financing)

Seller carry–back financing. So simple, so eloquent. So screwed up so often. This discussion is about seller carry–back from the sell side perspective. Most buyers are of the opinion that obtaining a seller carry–back is a good thing. Most sellers are confused on the matter thus refrain from its' consideration (as a confused mind always says no– to everything).

I recently drove by a national burger chain advertising their latest fare: a Turkey Jalepeno Burger. Now that's creative! Not very appetizing in my book, but creative. No doubt this offering is the product of hundreds of hours of market research and taste tests. It was probably first offered in just a few stores. If it has legs the product expansion will continue.

Mortgage loan products are developed in a similar way. If you recall, CMBS (Commercial Mortgage Backed Securities) is a relatively new mortgage product. The first tranche was not a billion dollar portfolio, more likely one hundred million, then tinkered with until deemed viable to sell to institutional investors.

How old is seller carry–back financing? Likely close behind ancient man's creation of language when the first farmer sold a developed field to another in exchange for a percentage of crops (for a period of time– of course). More likely after the invention of the abacus when bean counting transformed from hobby to profession.

The current day problem with seller carry–back financing is that most lending institutions are opposed to secondary financing. More succinctly, most financial institutions are opposed to non–institutional secondary financing. Mezzanine financing is fine on commercial deals where the first lien holder is involved in all layers wrapped into the mortgage.

## A Seller Carry–back that works

A seller carry–back that works for the seller is when equity in the deal equates to at least twenty percent (20%) and the amount carried–back by the seller is less than one third (33%) of the senior mortgage financing.

Good Example: Deal strike price is $1,000,000. Cash down payment is $200,000, first mortgage is $600,000 with a seller carry–back of $200,000.

Why is this a good deal for the seller? Because it is a defensible position. There is equity behind the seller carry–back and a manageable first mortgage in front of the seller carry–back. If the seller had to foreclose on this position the mortgage financing in place at origination equates to a sixty percent (60%) loan–to–value of the originating purchase price.

## A Seller Carry–back that doesn't work

A seller carry–back that does not work for the seller, using the same dollar amount as in the prior transaction:

Bad Example: Deal strike price is $1,000,000. Cash down payment is $100,000, first mortgage is $800,000 with a seller carry–back of $100,000.

This is a precarious position for the seller carry–back mortgage. The likelihood of foreclosing on this position is improbable as even a successful foreclosure leaves the originating seller saddled with a property financed at 80% of the sales price. When considering a seller carry–back presume that you, the seller, will have to foreclose on the senior financing. Having sold the asset how many sellers have the mental stamina to take back this same deal highly levered? Very few. Thus, the carry–back goes up in smoke.

For a seasoned real estate investor doing so could be "just another deal" in the course of business. For the non–seasoned, having to proceed with a foreclosure to protect a secondary piece of financing deemed (by them) to be a valuable asset... this could be a life event. If so, avoid seller carry–back financing. For the seasoned, full steam ahead and please consider the rule of thumb presented here.

Another "trap" for sellers is when the only cause for using the carry–back is to overcome credit risk raised about the buyer. Here is where the scale of justice is in your hands. However, being a judge does not excuse you from being burned in the transaction. Becoming "the bank" brings with it all the rights and privileges of having to collect. Weigh carefully.

# Beauty in the Eyes of the Lien–holder

Like art, loans are sometimes critiqued as beautiful, ugly, abstract, well done or amateurish. Unlike in art, we use other words to describe mortgage loans; well secured, in compliance, in technical default, over–leveraged and exceeding disposition value. Who uses these words; the mortgagee, the lender.

It's true; mortgagees (lenders) are people too. Most are not real estate people, they are bankers, investment advisers or portfolio managers charged with protecting the assets within their respective portfolios. As lenders, it just so happens that many of the assets they invest in are real estate assets. Is this a contrary statement?

*Here is an old story: three men are blind–folded and an object is placed in their hands. They are asked to describe the object. The first man feels an object slender and moving like a snake; the second man has his arms wrapped around something so big it must be a tree trunk; the third man is holding a coarse object that is very long and "undone" at the end like a rope. The first man is holding an elephant's trunk, the second man the elephant's leg, the third man the elephants tail...*

It is important to recognize that a lender looks at your assets COMPLETELY differently than you do. As an owner we see real estate assets from facets that include; an operational business; a revenue producer; pride of ownership.

**Mortgage**: Security for a debt, or loan, utilizing real estate as collateral.

The vocabulary and language of the mortgagee is very different from the vocabulary and language of real estate investors. A mortgagee thinks in terms of:

**Lien–holder**: A right given to another by the owner of property to secure a debt.

**Return on equity**: A measure of how well a company reinvests earnings to generate additional earnings.

**Alienation clauses**: A clause in the loan documents that makes the loan due and payable if the property is transferred.

**Beneficiary**: Refers to the lender in a deed of trust.

**Liquidation value**: The probable price at a "forced sale", the fire sale price where reasonable market time is unlikely.

Ever hear a real estate owner discuss liquidation value with a smile? Probably not. Lenders are all about risk and protecting their investment, their cash. This is done through various levels of assessing risk, controlling risk, mitigating risk. And there are varying types of risk they look at: Market risk, asset risk, strength of borrower.

One example of the perfect real estate deal from a lender's perspective is new construction, very, very low loan–to–value with an extremely high debt service coverage ratio and high reserves. And this deal is only one in a hundred that lenders get to consider.

Investor bread–and–butter deals are mortgage lenders bread–and–butter deals. When seeking financing the matter at hand is to determine the type of bread and what flavored jelly, as this changes from one lender to the next.

As a borrower, it is your responsibility equally with the lender to identify whether or not the deal you are seeking to finance or re–finance fits into the lenders "box." If yes, then great. Respond to lender inquiries that compel the lender to continue towards a loan closing. Keep in mind that although you and your lender are discussing the same deal, the perspective on risk, the vocabulary and objectives diverge all along the way.

# Chapter 5

## Opinion & Editorial

# Five Low Tech Business Gadgets That Work

Going "low tech" in business? What a concept! In an era where "apps" response times are measured in nanoseconds, what chance does a low tech gadget have in this environment to promote your business?

In an average day, how many emails, text and tweets do you review before getting out of bed in the morning? Don't say you're not checking. If not, it's only because your significant other is giving you "that look." For others, both people are checking their phones, even before their feet hit the ground in the morning. Welcome to America.

Are there alternatives to this? Are there a few "old school" tactics that still have relevancy? I'm glad you ask. Here are a few:

**The telephone**. While almost every business is loaded to the gills with wi–fi and wires, we have at our disposal that old technology built in the late 1800's and still kicking around today: voice. Email is great, texts have their place, but sometimes a simple telephone call will get more done than 22 back–and–forth texts ever will. Try it. I bet there is still one sitting on your desk.

**Post It's®**. In business, record keeping is important. We want paper trails and completed files. However, sometimes a simple Post It note is all that's necessary to move a project or file to the next step. They are also wonderful for same day or next day reminders.

**A handshake**. Who gets up from a meeting without looking down at their phone to see what they missed whilst being "stuck" in a meeting with real people? Remember eye contact? Remember handshakes? Remember small talk at the end of meeting; that point of departure where sometimes the "real meeting" begins?

**Listening**. Multitasking be damned. Try doing one thing at one time. And the hardest thing of all is to listen. I mean really listen to the person you are in conversation with for the entire time of the engagement. It could very well be thirty or sixty minutes. I know you can do it! Your ears will not start bleeding.

**Thank you notes**. Snail mail remains a personal touch that has unfortunately become passe' leaving this art form to those who actually care. People receive so few personal notes, hand written notes, that when one does arrive it is truly memorable.

Four of the five "low tech gadgets" require no electronics. All have a very low carbon footprint so there is limited guilt that using them is adding to the eventual demise of the human race. Further more, each of these endeavors can be done with coffee. How good is that?

# Multifamily French Fries
## (A Fragmented Marketplace)

Multifamily assets are like french fries; everyone thinks theirs are the best. But with so many to choose from how do you know? The multifamily marketplace is a fragmented industry. No one entity or person owns a controlling interest.

McDonald's buys more potatoes and sells more french fries than anyone. However, knowing who makes and sells the most french fries (or beer, or boots) has not deterred others. And there is always room for one more.

Biggest is represented by a single number. Best in class is more subjective. Multifamily is a fragmented industry as the biggest firms in the industry control less than one percent of assets.

The 50 biggest multifamily owners in the United States own and control approximately 2,700,000 housing units. That's a big number. However, it represents only two percent (2%) of the total housing market. That's right, just two percent.

Who owns the most multifamily units in the United States? Boston Capital with 158,000 units. In second place is Centerline Capital Group with 152,000 units. These are big, well capitalized companies. Yet if these two companies doubled in size tomorrow they would not own one tenth of one percent of the housing market.

We've all met people who own a single rental house or duplex who can talk for an hour about their view on property management. Hey, they are part of the industry too.

And who knows, five years from now this person may own ten or twenty rentals. They are part of our fragmented industry. The founder will be the hardest working property manager you know.

# Housing and the Evolution of Mankind

Some of the oldest continuously inhabited housing in the United States is in Taos, New Mexico, where there are pueblos continuously inhabited for almost 1,000 years (smithsonian.com May 2012).

In the history of mankind, housing has evolved to include structures of every conceivable shape. We have lived under trees, in caves, built hovels and established movable, nomadic cities in deserts and on prairie lands. But wait, there's more!

Our home building skills have evolved to the point that certain countries have a surplus of houses. Talk about nailing the technology.

Question? What century are we discussing? Was there ever, in the history of mankind, a housing surplus prior to financial engineering? Or are housing construction surpluses a modern economic happenstance exclusively?

Historically, there were several incidences of surplus housing. Most times had to do with disease wiping out huge portions of the in–place population. Or forced migration caused by war or famine.

In modern times surpluses are often caused by job dislocation– jobs moving from one metro to another metro (as when a large auto manufacturer relocates).

Anyone following U.S. housing starts through the recession can identify the precipitous drop in new construction. I believe this lack of construction is playing out in the rental market today with higher rent growth, and will play out tomorrow with a shortage of available housing.

The beginning of "tomorrow" is now. One reason for the delay is the egregious time devoted to clear homes in various stages of foreclosure. These foreclosures will clear. When foreclosures come on the market inforce it will appear, momentarily, as if the U.S. has a surplus of housing. And then they will be gone. This is a one–time shot of inventory.

In a recent interview on Bloomberg, Professor Case (of the Case Shiller Index) stated that housing starts are now one third of the peak from when construction was adding over $600B to Gross Domestic Product (GDP).

Prof. Case stated than even today, one quarter to one third of homes remain "under water" with mortgage balances exceeding home values. Case noted, concurrently, that construction starts remain below the level necessary to replace housing removed from service and below the level necessary to keep pace with population growth.

The elasticity of this rubber band will burst in a year or two as housing starts remain below levels necessary to replace dwellings lost through atypical means; such as fire, flood, disrepair and age.

As the saying goes "It's hard to dig yourself out of a hole." The same applies to a soon–to–be shrinking housing stock.

# Living in a 2% GDP World

I have a friend who is an investment advisor. He rails often against the extended amount of time, energy and effort placed before us via the media as to whether or not the quarterly gross domestic product (GDP) of the United States will come in at a 1.9% annual rate vs. 2.1%. His patent response is "very few people are making investment decisions based on that differential."

**Gross Domestic Product** is the total market value of all final goods and services produced in a country in a given year, equal to the total consumer, investment and government spending plus the value of exports minus the value of imports (www.InvestorsWords.com)

Large components of the economy can swing GDP a few tenths or more in a given year. Housing, auto manufacturing, airline and defense are four such components.

**Housing**. Housing is but one part of GDP that has failed live up to its historic response. Housing is relied on to add jobs during recovery. This time the laws of supply and demand have taken precedence. Although supply is underwhelming, demand is diminished, hampered by a stubborn unemployment rate, consumer rebalancing of their personal balance sheets and a narrowing of the credit window. Commonly used credit quality scores for mortgage qualifications are a historic footnote in today's mortgage marketplace.

**Auto manufacturing**. The auto industry has shrunk to a shadow of itself as compared to prerecessionary times. The industry once produced almost fifteen million units per year. Now that number is closer to twelve million. But these lower levels are more profitable based on industry restructuring and a change in product outputs to more fuel efficient models (reflecting higher fuel prices).

The "ace–in–the–hole" for auto manufacturers is that they can offer their own in-house financing. This gives dealerships a tool allowing auto sellers to pull demand forward, or more succinctly, create demand. With the average age of auto stock in the U.S. being almost eleven years, people want new product. Obtaining this new product is occurring based on dealer financing.

**Airline manufacturing**. The airline industry is hugely capital intensive. The sale of commercial jetliners around the world can represent a few tenths of a percent in U.S. GDP every quarter. Airline seat capacity has decreased in recent years as older, less fuel -efficient planes are taken out of service. Less capacity also allows airlines to take price. Recently, Boeing has released a new airliner that offers significant fuel savings. This as the airline executives groan at the duel mandate of reducing fuel usage and controlling capital expenditures. The bait (fuel savings) is just too good to pass up to not look at buying a younger, more fuel efficient fleet.

**Defense Spending**. I do not pretend to understand the defense industry other than to comment that it has a significant effect on GDP. One fact we have is that the U.S. was engaged in two wars but is no longer. Does this fact reduce defense spending? I pray we do not require the outbreak of war to justify defense spending increases.

# Interior Design: Home Office Workspace

Multifamily interior design is in constant motion. Changing with the times, new designs reflect the necessity of energy conservation and "at home" work space. Home office workspace, while still on the kitchen table all too often, has moved to a permanent space as modern multifamily designs include home office workspace. Sometimes this is a nook, othertimes a room with full connectivity set up for what seems like space flight from the second bedroom.

How soon until the place we call work and the place we call home are the exact same place? Do we really want to work from "home" as a society? Sustainable cities are devoting larger portions of their shrinking budgets to creating transportation districts, centralized living and working environments that reduce the need for motorized transportation. Is this evolution dissolving the already vague line between work and home?

We are only 100 years removed from dirt roads. Now we travel on electronic highways going faster and further in a single day than our grandparents could circumnavigate in a lifetime. The federal government and private sector have expanded "work from home" policies exponentially in recent years. These policies reduce the need for office buildings and time commuting. Home offices are referred to as family friendly and remote site, among other names.

The Romans were dedicated to creating sustainable roads throughout their kingdom, a kingdom that spanned a continent and beyond. But it was an Englishman who established roads that could withstand harsh use and all weather.

Now we travel throughout the country and around the world through a wire that carries electronic pulses and "packages" of information. More often, we travel with no wire at all using bandwidth and spectrum. How will this change the place we call "home" and the place we call "work?"

It was President Truman who initiated the federal highway program beginning construction in St. Louis, Missouri on a highway across the country-from sea to shining sea. The highway was named after his predecessor, President Eisenhower.

How many offices do you personally interact with? Corporate office, regional office, state office, metro office, car office, hot spot, laptop, cloud, smart phone. And, home office; gotta have that too. Are we all insane? Is there an app for that?

I remember getting my first laptop from my employer back when this was high–tech (weight ten pounds). I was so excited. My boss looked at me grimly stating, "So now you know this means we expect you to work 24/7."

We have turned our televisions into e–machines and cell phones into MS Office mini–suites to edit documents and e–sign changes. Like the six–million dollar man, how long until we can no longer tell the difference between human and artificial intelligence?

While deciding this point, consider that between 10–20% of people work from home on a full time basis. And the other 80% work from home some of the time during their work week. Home office environments continue to evolve into fully functional work space offices. The multifamily industry must adapt to this seachange.

Providing secure wireless is, anymore, just a starting point of "business services" to a residence. It's a brave new technological world. Electronic interconnectivity will increase as asphalt roads to and from work, continue to become slow moving parking lots.

# Multifamily Devaluation (When Pigs Fly)

Pigs don't fly and functional multifamily assets seldom trade at a significant discount to replacement costs. Soon after TARP (Troubled Asset Recovery Program) was implemented in 2008 the sharks circled, eyeing bundles of multifamily assets presumed to hit the market at distressed prices... fire sale prices. The sale never happened. Why? Because pigs don't fly.

Why is it so hard to devalue multifamily assets? One reason is their popularity– the asset class has legs. Thus, even an upside down owner believes to their core that valuations will return "any minute" (note to self; market timing never works– see Gartman Interest Rate Observer) www.grantspub.com.

In the fall of 2008 credit markets froze, we learned about TARP and elected a new president. As a HUGE problem is apt to do, TARP did little that connected with its name as few "troubled assets" were purchased with this government program. But we are still here, minus a depression, so there were some significant positives to the intervention.

It is common for multifamily assets to trade at 80% of "replacement value." Appraisals are a necessary part of our business. A third–party valuation is intended to provide an unbiased "opinion of value." We rely on these opinions to trade and finance assets. Appraisals often provide a cross section of valuation methods; market value and cost approach (sometimes referred to as replacement value).

*Replacement Value: The value of an asset as determined by the estimated cost of replacing it.*

The value on multifamily assets is based on their ability to earn "X" dollars. Replacement value often times gets in the way. Here is where you get the uneasy feeling that surely this asset should have a higher valuation based on the cost to replace it.

As much as real estate asset prices are directly connected to revenue and NOI, replacement value is an underlying support to price and perceived value. Is it the only one? Of course not, but it acts as a constant reminder that requires buyers and sellers to think beyond just income and expenses.

Land has value, structures have value. Replacement value refers to the cost of replacing buildings (or structures). We rightfully assume the costs of "new" construction is greater than the cost of original construction; wood, drywall, roofing, fixtures, cabinets, labor, overhead, insurance. In current dollars, all of these components of construction cost more today than they did yesterday (or one year ago, or ten years ago).

Property values last peaked in 2007. The recession started prior to the collapse of Lehman in the Fall of 2008. In that window (spring 2007 to summer 2008) cap rates were compressed, mortgage money flowed and multifamily transaction volume was at record levels.

Waiting around for multifamily prices to drop to some level far below replacement value is, in essence, a big waste of time. Companies large and small waited for this event with intentions of scooping up assets for pennies on the dollar. It never happened.

From 2009 forward thousands of multifamily mortgages were in technical default, but the banks had bigger problems to address–things like assuring their very survival. The possibility of foreclosing *en masse* on thousands of commercial assets was more than a daunting thought; it was impractical. The prospect of collecting "bad assets" for resale in an era of such instability was beyond the bounds of reasonable thought.

To find the answer to the question as to when multifamily assets prices will drop through the floor... see the title of this article.

# Multifamily Administration: Tax Counsel

Behind every successful multifamily asset stands good counsel, both legal and tax. One statement that is absolutely true about tax counsel: If you don't call, they can't help.

Tax counsel is money well spent. Engaging a firm with full time tax professionals assures your circumstances receive the benefits from counsel that is aware of current tax law and best practices. Tax strategy is not about filling out forms; tax strategy takes into account the application of current tax code as it relates to your financial state of affairs.

Even with stabilized multifamily assets the pace of change in tax law can be overwhelming. A buy and hold strategy that has a ten or twenty year ownership objective can be severely tempered based on changes in tax law.

Too many people believe your lawyer should stand at the ready (24/7) and your accountant should be called April 14. In fact, contacting your accountant on January 2 is too late as any recommended changes cannot be accomplished because the tax year is now over. Tax planning is a year–long process that takes into account the changing nature of aggregate circumstances of individual assets affecting your tax consequences.

In a recent article by Warren Buffett entitled, "Rich Can Afford a Tax Hike" he states the following: "...maybe you'll run into someone with a terrific investment idea who won't go forward with it because of the tax he would owe when it succeeds. Send him my way. Let me unburden him." Said another way, tax consequences should not stand in the way of making a sound investment decision.

Consider, please, making October "tax matters" review month. Maybe a new holiday for October 1 that we name "call my accountant" for coffee day. The point is to get ahead of tax matters prior to the end of year. You will be glad you did.

# What is Your Natural Next Step?

We all have one; that natural next step. The issue is choosing where to focus your steps, attention, mental energy and resources. Then there is balance; balancing personal and professional endeavors for a meaningful life. The best of all worlds is to make progress in our journey without fooling ourselves to assure that "activity" is not automatically perceived as progress.

There. Now that we have the self–help mambo jambo out of the way, let's talk. So. Question?

**Whatta ya wanna do next? And where? With whom? And for how long?**

**The where**. Part of determining your natural next step is determining the "where." Geography, weather, commute times, costs of living, costs of housing, schools, medical, etc. One of the outgrowths of our recent economic meltdown (and pending continuance) is that fewer people are moving from one metro to another. The primary driver of picking up and moving is a job change. Not much of that going on in the last few years as people have been content to maintain. Also, with fewer jobs and millions of underwater mortgages, there is less incentive to make a serious move without deep, and sometime tortuous thought. Sorry folks, no answers on this front. Just questions.

**With whom**. Professionally speaking, it's more fun to work with people you like. We hear all the time, "You don't get to choose your family." Does the same hold true in the workplace? When my wife, Dr. Della, is speaking to college kids about career options she always says "Remember to interview the employer while they are interviewing you– ask questions and meet potential colleagues." That's good advice for anyone job hunting.

**How long**. A career track, anymore, will include five to eight jobs. The probability that all of these jobs will be with the same employer is very small. People change jobs for all sorts of reasons; advancement, moving closer to family, a change of scenery. Some people plain get bored with their position, others have no place to move up within an organization. Give some thought as to how long you want to stay in a position. Give your self permission to consider other options from time to time along your career path.

I think when you find your "natural next step.".. it just feels right. You have that positive gut check thing going on. Yes, it's hard to measure warm and fuzzy. But this is much deeper. Look at the headings above. If you are in a geographic area you want to be in, working with people that care about the work and you can sketch out about how long you want to stay... then I think you have touched on three points to build a quality decision towards a self–selected, and balanced, quality of life.

Consider the following questions:

- *Question: How do you decide where you want to live, where you want to work?*

- *Question: When searching for a new job, what attributes are you looking for in colleagues?*

- *Question: What are the determining factors in how long you stay with your employer?*

# Multifamily and the Pace of Change

The average adult living in 1776 had less information available to them in their lifetime than what is provided to us today in a single Sunday copy of the New York Times. In 1865, the U.S. Civil War was practically over by the time knowledge of the war reached much beyond the shores of Europe. In the early 1900's American travelers to Africa were asked about "the great man Lincoln" as if he were still president.

Been to a construction materials conference lately? Recognize anything? Anything at all? Why replace a counter top when you can use a paint roller to cover the existing surface with material that has a granite–like finish?

Why carpet an entire room (ever again) when for less money you can install "carpet squares" allowing maintenance to replace only those areas of flooring that are worn or torn?

Have you seen the self–cleaning windows? Seems a bit of a stretch to me but no doubt the technology will be perfected in due time. What about elevators with 24–hour connect to service technicians who continuously monitor for irregularities?

And Wi–Fi. Sometimes I feel "so connected" my skin begins to crawl. Remember when "Tang" was all the rage because it was used in "outer space?"

At Oak Ridge National Laboratory (ornl.gov), the Department of Energy just notified the world–at–large that their newest super computer, Titan, has the capacity to perform twenty million calculations per second. Twenty million! Per second!

The real estate business can seem monolithic; we change on an as necessary basis when change is forced upon us. Well, change is being forced upon us at an ever increasing rate.

You think Craigslist is cool, what about property management software that creates and distributes your product across eighty websites with the click of a mouse (does anyone still have a wired mouse?).

For your own sanity it is better to adapt to change even if embracing it takes a while. Did you know that almost 25% of adults under the age of 25 have at least one tattoo? Change. It's here.

# Rents and the Poverty Trap

What is a poverty trap? Is there a solution to generational subsidized housing? Is subsidized housing passed down from one generation to the next? Does our society assist in perpetuating the poverty trap?

A poverty trap is "any self–reinforcing mechanism which causes poverty to persist." If it persists from generation to generation, the trap begins to reinforce itself if steps are not taken to break the cycle." (Wikipedia)

In the United States, poverty traps often include housing as part of the equation. More than one in ten rental households in America receive some form of rent subsidy.

Poverty traps are evident all over the world. A modern day example is when a community has no potable water or consistent source of food. It's easy for our minds to correlate that having to devote extensive time to finding food and water leaves limited energy for other endeavors. It's a simple economic paradigm.

Many believe rents are higher because of subsidized housing and the costs to construct, maintain and manage housing built to market rate standards. I disagree. If subsidized housing were built to a lower standard the costs to construct may be lower, but all other related costs remain the same (land costs, legal fees, setting utilities). The biggest difference is in the costs to society (and communities) with sub par housing having a much shorter term of functional use before necessary replacement.

There are three major federal rental assistance programs — the Housing Choice ("Section 8") voucher program, public housing, and the Section 8 project–based rental assistance program — as well as a handful of smaller programs, such as the Section 521 rural rental assistance program administered by the Department of Agriculture. Under existing funding levels, these programs can assist approximately 4.8 million low–income families. (Center for Budget and Policy Priorities www.cbpp.org)

Note the number of "families" – 4.8 million families. The Federal programs mentioned exclude Low Income Housing Tax Credits (LIHTC), state issued bonds, programs for seniors, those with disabilities, locally funded programs and charities. In total, tens of millions of people receive some form of rental assistance.

Does subsidized housing perpetuate a poverty trap? This is a hard question. Being in the multifamily business, we should engage in the conversation and help to shape policy and strategy. With such a huge number of people and resources in play, there is no single right answer, but many paths to assist in housing the greatest number of people with an eye towards making housing self–sufficiency a reality.

# Five Reasons Why People Rent Apartments

Many believe the only reason people rent multifamily apartments is because of housing affordability, meaning people only rent because they cannot afford to be home owners. This is simply not true. There are myriad reasons why people rent apartments. Following are just a few of those reasons.

**Convenience.** Apartment homes can provide varying types of convenience; close to work, easy commute to the city center, proximity to parks, etc. People define convenience in many ways. Convenience can be as simple as having the ability to make only a short–term commitment (one year lease vs. owning forever). Convenience can be keeping one's options open to other opportunities by being mobile.

When traveling by myself, I have a preference for full service hotels. When traveling with my family, I prefer extended stay hotels. Each offers a certain type of "convenience" With full service I can order in and keep working. At extended stay, if the kids want popcorn with the late night movie the microwave is right there next to the fridge. Each type of property offers certain conveniences depending on my needs. The same argument can apply to renting vs. owning.

**Location**. What's in an address? Do you live in Laguna Niguel or Anaheim? Queens or in the City? Oakland or Palo Alto? Is one place better than another? It depends on who you ask, right? Regardless of where we call work, many people are willing to commute to live in a place that meets their desired standard of living. Schools come into play, crime rates, public places, sure. But in their minds eye is finding a place that makes them feel good about themselves, their accomplishments, where they find themselves in life and comfort.

**Lifestyle**. Your perception is your reality. And with apartment homes these perceptions create a persona that generates differentiation based on amenities, size, style. In luxury properties, it is not uncommon to see fresh flowers in the lobby every day. Do people place fresh flowers in their home each day? Some do, but most do not. Yet a lifestyle property provides this amenity as part of your rental experience. People come to expect it and note its absence. Lifestyle.

**Price**. There can be significant differentials between the price of renting vs. buying. Yet even if the price were equal there are many who prefer to rent rather than own. Why? Some recognize the costs of ownership is a commitment beyond the initial purchase price. Taxes can increase, things break, neighborhoods change. Thus, price is only one of many reasons why a family may choose to rent.

**Financial flexibility**. In every price range there are home owners who have a mortgage with a balance higher than the property value. And sometimes prices go down (gasp! really?). So whereas home ownership, historically, was a great inflation hedge and potentially sound financial investment, most people are now firmly aware that equity is a gift and not a right (using the word gift very loosely).

Look at this short list without your "business brain". Notice that three of the five reasons people rent housing rather than buy housing is non–financial. Individuals and families rent for reasons other than just dollars and cents. Consider this factor when implementing your leasing and marketing plan.

# How Safe is Your Data?

Do you know who your data is dating? Unlike a clumsy teenager coming home after curfew, our data can sometimes be "out all night" and all day without anyone knowing. It only takes seconds for a security breach to become a major event.

Recently, a CBS news reporter noticed unusual behavior on her home–based work computer. Further investigation revealed that her computer had been hacked and that the perpetrators went through extraordinary lengths in an attempt to cover their tracts to avoid detection.

A recent Wired Magazine article claimed the "password is dead" and gave a dozen good reasons to believe it. Unfortunately, they provided limited alternatives to our present day quagmire of having to rely on a very small string of characters to protect access to our very large information data banks.

Consider also the Army private who provided thousands of sensitive documents to WikiLeaks all from a single laptop downloading on to CDs and flash drives. How do we control this? Like violent crime, very often the assailant is known to the victim and our data is made accessible to others by people we know. Thus, the first order of business is controlling access points and the people who must access your data.

Tim McCarver, one of the greatest baseball commentators (in my opinion), rails against people who would have umpires born and raised in certain cities from being able to call baseball games behind the plate in those cities. He breaks it down to its most common theme, stating "Everybody is from somewhere." His point being these are professionals, let them do their work.

When it comes to data security, engage the professionals who work in data security who can tell you down to the brass tacks how to defend your data, where and how to store your data and remove it from harm's way, whether the harm is man–made or an act of God. This is no place to guess. Let the professionals do their work.

Consider that data protection begins with determining who within your organization has categorical access. The likelihood is that number should be much smaller than exists today. Does every accountant at the firm performing your corporate and personal tax returns have access to your data? Probably not. Access is restricted to those who must have it to accomplish certain task. In property management, we know the whereabouts of each masterkey at all times. To the best of our ability the "keys" to our data and systems should be held to this same standard.

# Guns N' Butter and Housing

Is there a connection between war and when housing cycles recover in the greater economy? The guns vs. butter argument revolves around the theory that any society has limited resources.

While food (butter) is a necessity of life, we also need to protect the food we have (with guns) otherwise someone stronger will take away the food we have produced. It is good to grow food, and consume the food we grow without threat. We avoid being threatened by showing outsiders the ability to protect what we have.

Since the end of World War II housing formed as a stalwart in the guns n' butter paradigm. When the GI's came home they needed housing and jobs. Building housing created both housing stock and jobs. Financing the housing was necessary to make it all work. And it worked well.

**Is it true that when wars end housing flourishes?**

The United States for most of its short history is consistently in a state of either winding up for war or winding down from war.

Some people who fought in the Revolutionary War were still living at the beginning of the War of 1812. Some born during the time of this war were living during the U.S. Civil War in the 1860's. Some born during the Civil War fought in the Spanish–American War of 1898.

These conflicts are followed by World War I (1914–18), World War II (1939–44), The Korean War (1950–3), Vietnam (1965–74), Gulf War (1990–), Afghanistan (2001–) and the War on Terror (2001–).

Are we winding down from war today? If the answer is yes, then expect housing to flourish as domestic consumption takes center stage and fewer national resources are utilized around the globe to combat the enemy from afar.

# Guest Authors

# CraigsList Cold War

Author: Daniel Cunningham

I had a conversation the other day (at times a thinly–veiled argument) with a representative from an apartment listing publication which shall remain nameless, over the impact of Craigslist on the apartment publication industry. She refused to acknowledge the quality and volume of renter prospect traffic that can be generated by a Craigslist ad and couldn't even own her patently obvious disadvantage that the lease acquisition cost of Craigslist is zero and all other serious print/online pubs are, well, much more than that. I know she has to tow the party–line but at this point, if you're an apartment print magazine claiming you're as effective at driving traffic as Craigslist, especially when advertising costs are computed, then you're losing serious credibility.

For many property owners/managers, Craigslist is the alpha and omega of critical marketing activities. Personally, I don't have one community under Leonardo Management which couldn't thrive strictly off leads generated by Craigslist ads. I understand that during a lease–up or asset repositioning, a wider shotgun approach is necessary to try to reign in as many leads as possible in the shortest amount of time, even if the lease acquisition cost is high. For a stabilized community in a primary or secondary market, however, Craigslist is, without question, the "go–to."

This isn't to say that I fully understand this phenomenon. How can a site with a notoriously terrible user interface, a sorry excuse for search filtering, which is peppered throughout with listings that are sometimes completely uninformative at best and sometimes downright enigmatic at worst, become the consumer choice over the slicker, more search–friendly apartment hunting sites such as ForRent.com, Apartments.com, etc.? I understand Craigslist is a great place to find a used fridge, but the overwhelming use for apartment hunting popularity is confounding – although I do have a theory, and it is this: The very notion that Craigslist appears so unprofessional is what attracts consumers. The user's belief is there are deals to be had here – unsophisticated apartment owners and managers who just throw something up with rates below market and hope they get a phone call. Listings come like a ticker tape and if you're fast on the draw you might snag yourself home sweet home at a bargain. So those first page listings are gold – they have the smell of fresh opportunity and get swarmed like piranha bait.

The problem is, we on the apartment management side know this and we know the name of the game is to have your listings appear on that first page whenever possible. And so we have managers furiously posting ads two, three, ten times per day so the latest post can garner more traffic. Craigslist knows we do this, and rightly feels it degrades the value of their listing service to have the same unit appear a million times a day and so they in turn are constantly introducing new defenses against this behavior. They scan for repetitive language, posts from matching emails or even IP addresses. They have random phone call verification requirements and in extreme examples, they blacklist an entire company. In response, a cottage industry devoted to helping management companies skirt these defenses (for a fee) has sprouted up. "Secret" methods for fooling Craigslist are whispered around apartment networking groups like forbidden arcana. Thus was born, the Craigslist version of the cold war.

Here's the rub. The more successful we get at defeating Craigslist and flooding folks with our listings, the less useful Craigslist will become to users. And the harder Craigslist becomes to post available units the more management companies will have to turn towards the old guard of apartment search sites. In other words, unless Craigslist completely retools their interface to solve this tension, a collapse seems imminent.

If I were the "other" sites out there I would be looking keenly at positioning myself to be the heir apparent in a post–Craigslist era. I'm not sure what the better mousetrap is, but I know it would be some combination of ease of use in order to achieve broad apartment owner penetration combined with ability to push the right apartment to the right person, likely through some combination of social networking and Yelp–like tools. I am available to consult on an hourly basis.

In the meantime, your reward for reading this whole post is that I'm going to give you, the apartment owner, the most powerful and effective weapon ever invented to defeat the Craigslist defense shield. Properties where our own Craigslist posting efforts garnered us 8–10 calls per day have seen that volume double or even triple through this service (which validates the thesis that successful multiple postings are good as gold.) I hesitate to even share it, because I know the more widely used it becomes, the more of Craigslist's attention it will receive and eventually they will find a way to defeat it. But for now, go to http://www.rentlogicleads.com/, sign up as quick as you can, send me a personal "thank you" once you're up and running, and tell Gregg he owes me one. That's all I'm going to say about it. Happy posting and good hunting.

*Leonardo Management, Inc., is a commercial property management firm servicing multifamily, office, and retail properties & portfolios throughout California, Arizona, and Nevada. Visit www.leonardomgmt.com or keep pace on Twitter or our blog, LeoMgmtNews.*

# Real Estate Investment Alphabet – Part I

Author: Frank Gallinelli

It may seem like a witch's brew of random letters – but truly, it's just real estate investing. You can handle it. Any or all of these measures can be useful to you, if you understand what they mean and when to use them.

## NPV (Net Present Value)

NPV is, of course, Net Present Value. NPV is connected to what all good real estate investors and appraisers do, namely discounted cash flow analysis (aka DCF, if you'd like some more initials). Discounted cash flow is a pretty straightforward undertaking. You project the cash flows that you think your investment property will achieve over the next 5, 10, even 20 years.

NPV is a method to pause and ponder the future value of an investment made with today's dollars.

Then you pause and remind yourself that money received in the future is less valuable than money received in the present. So, you discount each of those future cash flows by a rate equal to the "opportunity cost" of your capital investment. The opportunity cost is the rate you might have earned on your money if you didn't spend it to buy this particular property. Now you have the Present Value of all the future cash flows.

What does that mean to you as an investor? If the NPV is positive, it suggests that the investment may be a good one. That's because a positive NPV means the property's rate of return is greater than the rate you identified as your opportunity cost. The more positive it is in relation to the initial investment, the more inclined you'll be to accept this investment. Our result here is not stellar, but it is at least positive.

If the NPV is negative, the property returns at a rate that is less than your opportunity cost, so you should reject this investment and put your money elsewhere.

Clearly, the NPV here is very sensitive to changes in the discount rate. If you revise your thinking just slightly about the appropriate discount rate, then the conclusion you draw may likewise need to be revised. As little as a half–point difference could change your attitude from luke–warm to hot or cold. The prudent investor will test a range of reasonable discount rates to get a sense of the range of possible results.

While we're beating up on NPV, let's also note that it doesn't do you much good if your goal is to compare alternative investments. To have some kind of meaningful comparison, you need at least to keep the holding period for both properties the same. But what if one property requires a $300,000 cash investment, but the alternative investment requires $400,000? Fortunately, NPV has a cousin that can help you with that problem: Profitability Index.

## Profitability Index

While the NPV is the difference between the Present Value of future cash flows and the amount you invested to acquire them, Profitability Index is the ratio. It doesn't tell you the number of dollars; it tells you how big the return is in proportion to the investment.

A Profitability Index of exactly 1.00 means the same as an NPV of zero.

You're looking at two identical amounts, in one case divided by each other so they give a result of 1.00 and in the other case subtracted one from the other, equaling zero.

An Index greater than 1.00 is a good thing, the investment is expected to be profitable; an Index less than 1.00 is a loser. When you compare two investments, you expect the one with the greater Index to show the greater profit.

**But Wait...**

This sounds terrific; we've found the perfect way to measure our investment's return. But wait – Internal Rate of Return (IRR) has a few warts. Sometimes its results are imperfect, sometimes even misleading. In Part II, we will look at the problems with IRR and at some potential solutions. We'll examine Modified IRR and Capital Accumulation Comparison (CpA), and how they might provide us with a means of dealing with the shortcomings.

(Reprinted with permission of RealData — software for real estate investors and developers —realdata.com)

# Real Estate Investment Alphabet – Part II

Author: Frank Gallinelli

## IRR (Internal Rate of Return)

Internal Rate of Return (IRR) seems to befuddle many investors, but if you understand Discounted Cash Flow and Net Present Value, then you already understand IRR. That's because it is really the same process, but one where you are solving for a different unknown.

In Discounted Cash Flow (DCF), you believe you know what the future cash flows will be, and you believe you know the rate at which those cash flows should be discounted. Your mission is to figure the Present Value of the cash flows.

With IRR, you still believe you know what the future cash flows will be, but now you know the Present Value (PV) and want to find the discount rate. How is it that you know the Present Value? This is a deal happening in the real world. The PV is the amount of cash you are paying for those future cash flow. When you solve for the IRR, you are looking for the discount rate that accurately describes the relationship between those future cash flows and the money you put on the table on Day One.

When you've found the discount rate that makes the PVs of the future cash flow equal to your initial investment, you've found the IRR. You can express this another way:

**When you've found the discount rate that makes the NPV equal zero, you've found the IRR.**

Admittedly, the math to find the IRR is ugly, but if you're reading this then you probably have a computer (or a highly sensitive gold filling that also picks up the BBC); there are plenty of tools, including Microsoft Excel and our own RealData software that will do the job for you.

**IRR is the measurement of choice for many investors because it takes into account both the timing and the magnitude of your cash flows.**

IRR is indeed sensitive to both the timing and amount of cash flow. Receipt of cash flows early in the investment cycle are especially valuable because you didn't have to wait long to receive them and therefore you didn't have to discount their values so greatly. This makes for a higher IRR, a higher yield on invested dollars.

(Reprinted with permission of RealData — software for real estate investors and developers — realdata.com)

# It's a Great Time to be a Borrower

Author: David Garfinkel

All of our capital sources are lending, and that is a good thing. Fannie/Freddie and HUD are lending to historic levels, and that is without as much acquisition activity as normal. The fact that CMBS is back is a good thing, as this has opened up a new channel of capital back into the marketplace. CBMS will lend on all property types and still has attractive debt. The hope is that these lenders can pickup loans that a life insurance company may not bid as aggressively for, including loans where leverage needs to be pushed or in markets that aren't major metropolitan areas.

The big question is when are interest rates going to go up? Since we are at historic lows, there is a lot of speculation that interest rates will rise. But when? They have been very low for quite a while. With the economic woes of Greece and Spain, and an upcoming election, many people don't think rates are going to move anytime in the near future. What does that mean for you the borrower? Take advantage now while rates are still low. If you can't make a deal work at these rates, then it isn't a good deal. One has to assume that eventually, rates will start to climb, and then the next question is where will they stop.

It is still important to note that the fundamentals of underwriting are still very important. Lenders aren't pushing leverage. They are really evaluating each loan as it relates to location, lease rollover, borrower strength and many other factors as they relate to making a real estate loan. But if the fundamentals work, then you should be able to take advantage of some of the lowest long–term rates that we have ever seen. As stated above, it is a great time to be a borrower.

Please note, David Garfinkel is a NorthMarq Capital employee and the views and opinions above are his alone and do not represent the official views of the company.

# Multifamily Capital Markets, Interrupted

Author: David Garfinkel

There is more capital in the marketplace today than since 2007. Many investors are trying desperately to get their money into real estate. Many lenders have increased their allocations and are looking to lend on quality real estate projects.

So who is lending? First, Fannie Mae and Freddie Mac were directed to cut back their lending 10%. Decreasing loan volume by 10% is still is a top–tier lending year for them. Will they become more selective? Yes, they probably will.

Who will benefit from this? The Life insurance companies and conduits. Life insurance companies have become major players for lending on multifamily projects and directly compete with Fannie Mae and Freddie Mac. They are consistently winning lower leverage loans and loans where the terms are not the typical 10–year product. If a borrower wants 5, 7, 12, or 15–year or longer money, the loan will likely go to a life insurance company.

Let's not forget HUD. If you want a 35–year fixed rate loan and have some patience, the HUD loan rates are still extremely attractive. The operative word here is "patience."

If you are looking for new debt there couldn't be a better time to take your loan to market. If you are looking to refinance a property or an acquisition preparation is a key to your success. Create a file with the last three years' income and expense information, a trailing 12-month breakdown, current rentroll, ownership chart/info and be prepared to answer questions.

A lot of due diligence goes into a loan, but with historically low interest rates it certainly is worth the time and effort. So if you are ready, it certainly continues to be a great time to be a borrower.

David can be reached at dgarfinkel@northmarq.com.

# "Real Life" Listings Matter

Author: Ryan Green

As our culture becomes increasingly more web based, it's easy to focus advertising listings all online. Services such as Craigslist and social media are great tools but they are just a single point of marketing for potential residents.

Because of the easy accessibility and large quantity of online listings, a physical listing in your area might stand out to prospective residents. This also means you're going to have to make it really stand out to be taken seriously.

### Newspaper Listings

Most classifieds listings that charge by the word or column inch provide a very limited amount of words or characters to work with based on costs. This means you need to sell your rental in a succinct matter. The best way to start writing a newspaper classified is by picking out a few keywords you believe describes your rentals. You will need to highlight the basics (rent, how many bedrooms, utilities, etc.). If you can spare the space, try to include at least one dynamic feature to the listing. This might include: gym access for apartment complexes, waterfront view, convenient location to landmark, etc.

Including a photo will make your listing much more appealing

It's also important to consider that an older audience is more likely to read the classifieds in the newspaper as younger generations are more prone to go directly to the Internet. Older renters tend to, but not always, have better credit scores and rental history than younger renters who have not had time to build up these credentials.

### Flyers and Signs

Flyers advertising rentals can be a dime a dozen, many opting just to put a picture with Times New Roman text underneath on white copy

152

paper. While a flyer should be professional, that doesn't mean it has to be drab and boring.

Utilizing photos of the rental is important for a successful flyer; try including samples of a select few rooms (possibly furnished). Try not to overwhelm the flyer with too many photos and *avoid* using clip art.

High quality photos will include a nice border and a few subtle accent colors to make your flyer stand out amongst the multitude of others out there. For fonts, avoid types such as Papyrus and Comic Sans. Stick with professional and clear fonts like Helvetica. Posting these around community boards by grocery stores and parks will make them stand out.

**Oldest and Newest Advertising Mediums**

While it may go along with Internet listings, Quick Response codes (QR) can be a fun way to get people interested in your property. QR codes are similar to bar codes but are scanned by apps on smart phones that redirect them to a link. These codes can be made for free on websites such as Kaywa. Posting these codes around your town alongside some text referring to rental listings might intrigue people to seek it out. You can also simply include QR codes on the bottom of your flyers if that is easier.

Radio still works. If you own a property management firm, you can advertise on local radio to let the public know about multiple listings.

All Property Management is a service to connect property owners to property managers. APM's database lets you search for local property managers in your region and get free quotes. www.allpropertymanagement.com.

# Finding the Best Renters: By the Numbers

Author: Ryan Green

A recent study of Experian RentBureau data found that more than 50,000 renters who initiated their leases over a six year period ended their leases owing money. Industry experts convened during the National Apartment Association Education Conference to analyze the study of more than 750,000 U.S. renters of class A & B properties. Several findings concluded very surprising results.

## The Majority of Renters Have Credit Scores Below 700

While looking over a credit report to see where an applicant's score places them within the rental criteria, the majority of applicants may not meet the requirement on score alone. And, 56% of all applicants sampled had a score below 700[1].One reason for the high percentage of lower scores may be attributed to the fact that "Generation Y" (18 – 29 years old) who account for a critical audience in the rental market, comprise more than half of the applicants in the sample set.

When looking at the complete picture, this doesn't always demonstrate poor credit history, but instead could be attributed to a lack of time spent building a credit rating. This represents another reason to utilize more than just a score for applicant screening; check to see if the person has ever been evicted. Also, check past rental payment history; do they pay their rent on time?

## Two Skips Means Six Times the Risk

Following are three significant points to ponder:

1. It may not be too surprising that a renter who has missed a payment in the past may miss one again in the future. However, a defaulting renter can be substantially more accurately predicted during the resident screening process based on specific red flags. The experian study showed that while applicants with positive rental payment histories may have

nearly a 6% default rate, renters with two or more prior debts run a rate nearly 6 times that (of 35%).[1]

2. An applicant with two or fewer late or NSF payments on a report on their record showed nearly an 8% rate of default. Those applicants from the same sample who showed three or more late or NSF payments skyrocketed up to a nearly 17% default rate. Data from this objective perspective shows that while not everyone will have a pristine record, there is a defined line of when an applicant becomes a high risk.

3. The housing industry is laden with rules and regulations in place to protect both the lessee and the lessor. The best way for all parties to benefit is to find the most consistent procedures that everyone can understand and adhere to. While this may not always favor the applicant who has not kept up with maintaining the cleanest of backgrounds, the goal is to encourage and aide in promoting a positive lifestyle. By offering methods of building credit history such as making payments on time there becomes an added incentive benefiting both the renter and landlord.

You may view the complete analysis by visiting the Experian RentBureau website.

*Ryan Green has been in the housing industry for nearly 10 years working in various roles. He has both FCRA and Experian Certifications in Resident Screening. www.cicreports.com and* Yardi Software. To learn more about CIC visit their website at www.cicreports.com

---

1 For the purpose of this data analysis, Experian RentBureau utilized the VantageScore® advanced credit scoring model, which produces a highly predictive score and scores up to 14 million more consumers previously deemed unscoreable. VantageScore has a scale range of 501 to 990 to represent a consumer's credit worthiness.

# Preparing for Disaster

Author: Ryan Green

In the wake of numerous natural disasters over the last decade, it has become sadly obvious that a large majority of the world is not only unprepared for the worst, but remains unconcerned at the possibility of being struck by a natural disaster. Granted it's understandable when natural disasters hit at random, however, as a major communal threat, it is imperative that your properties have an emergency backup plan available. In aiming for the safety of your residents, staff, and assets, here are a few key points to consider when preparing your emergency plan:

**The Physiological Backup:** One of the most notable aspects when preparing for the worst, the physiological backup, deals with stockpiling basic supplies (such as water, canned foods, batteries, flashlights, matches, etcetera). This factor, while apparent when extended towards residents, is also needed towards staff. Is your property equipped to aid, not only your residents, but also your staff should they be required to remain on site?

**The Physical Backup:** Whether or not this tip is already known, it is still important to stress the usefulness of having some staff who are cross trained. Little thing matters—such as where they keep important documents, passwords might be to access records, and where they store their list of vendor contacts—will go a long way during a crisis.

**The Vendor Backup:** In addition to staff adapting to an emergency plan, vendors should be able to accommodate as well. In the event of a natural disaster, your vendors should be able to answer questions, taking care of your needs in a timely manner. Do your vendors have a response plan?

**Digital Backup**: With so much reliance on electronic storage and service, do you know if your data is secure? You and your vendor's digital data should be available not simply on–site, but elsewhere in order to make restoration during the aftermath progress seamlessly. As one such data company, CIC utilizes multiple emergency plans. With different sites across the country, we are able to keep our systems online should one region be affected in any way.

Of course, it's daunting to prepare for such a significant and lengthy plan, as the ambiguity of what and when it might strike is endless. Yet it's still inevitable that a natural phenomenon will affect your properties in some way. And just as a crisis strikes (as if Pandora's Box had leaked open), you'll appreciate taking the time to create a backup plan because in the end, that plan will equal hope.

*Ryan Green has been in the housing industry for nearly 10 years working in various roles. He has both FCRA and Experian Certifications in Resident Screening. www.cicreports.com*

# Pest Management in Multifamily

Author: Rose McMillan

Pest management is part of property management. There are a number of insects and small animals that can infest a multifamily home, and before you know it, the problem spreads and people are leaving in droves. If you are a responsible property manager, you must know how to deal with the situation, as well as how to prevent it in the first place.

There are numerous pests that can infest multifamily housing. Roaches, bedbugs, and rodents are just some of the primary offenders. Following are some important facts to keep in mind as you consider pest control:

**Education.** To make sure that you keep your building as pest free as possible, spend some time educating your residents. Print up an educational fact sheet. You can place these in your "new resident" packet. This is not to make your residents suspect a problem when there isn't one– it's education and preparedness. You are telling residents that if there is ever an issue, that you, the property manager, are prepared to address it.

**No–Fault Reporting**. Some residents are hesitant to report small pests problems because they are afraid they will be blamed. This can allow a small problem to spread until it is a major one. Instead, make it very clear that people who report problems will not be accused, evicted or otherwise punished. Emphasize that reported pests problems will be solved, without blame.

**Maintenance Pest Control.** Consider contracting with a local exterminator who you can work with, and put together a pest maintenance schedule. In some cases, the best defense is a good offense. There are some very mild pesticides that can be put down that will discourage pests of all types from entering your building in the first place. Take some time to think about what kind of procedures you want to institute. Regular spraying in certain key spots can make things a lot easier for your asset in the long run. Discuss what options will suit your situation best with your exterminator.

**Stay Diligent.** Many good property management habits can keep your buildings pest free. Encourage your residents to ask maintenance staff to fix drips and holes. Holes allow insects and mammals to crawl in, while drips encourage insects that are drawn to water. Make sure you fix any torn screens that you see, and that you seal cracks in places like the kitchen and the bathroom when you are dealing with newly-vacated units. In addition, make sure the brush around the property is trimmed back from building walls, as this will help prevent outdoor pests from getting inside.

**Treat Immediately.** When it comes to pest management, it is always better to treat an issue sooner rather than later. If you can fix a problem while it is still small, you have a much better chance of addressing it completely. Pest control is something that takes both time and effort, so be sure that you get a head start if you can.

Make sure your multifamily units stays pest free, take steps to be prepared. These preventative measures can save you from high expenses and frustrating months down the line.

Rose McMillan is an experienced pest control professional from Long Island, NY. Contact email: rosemcmillan573@gmail.com or Twitter: @pwipm_rose. References and resources provided by Terminix Library.

# Index

## R

Renewals  20, 34, 60, 73
Rental Revenue  36
Rent Growth  4, 6, 34, 36, 45, 46, 82, 85, 98, 101, 102, 121
Revenue  26, 30, 35, 36, 38, 40, 41, 42, 46, 47, 48, 60, 69, 89, 115, 128, 167

## S

Secondary Market  142
Software  31, 35, 133, 147, 148, 149
Submarket  3, 73, 81, 91, 92, 97, 98

## T

Tertiary  4, 11, 82
Tile  50, 51, 52
Turnover  20

## U

Underwriting  36, 150
Utilities  37, 42, 93, 134, 152
Utility  31, 69

## V

Vacancy  41, 42, 43, 45, 46, 47, 48, 82, 89, 98
Vinyl  50, 51

John Wilhoit, Jr.

# RENT ROLL TRIANGLE

Collected Rents

Stated Lease Rents

Gross Potential Rents

A three-step process to performing evidence-based due diligence of rental property income

**RentRollTriangle.com**

# Introduction to Rent Roll Triangle

Real estate investing is all about compartmentalizing risk. The better you are at this the better your investment decisions. Few people invest their money without a presumed yield in mind. The Rent Roll Triangle (RRT) assists in compartmentalizing strengths and weaknesses in rental revenue and identifying areas of concern pre-acquisition.

The rent roll is the focal point of determining value. That is what makes rent roll analysis so important.

This is a specialty book for people involved in the acquisition and management of rental property. USE WITH CAUTION. Mastery of the concepts will make you feel as if you have superior knowledge and the ability to time the market. I have never met anyone that can successfully time the market- any market, the exception being Sam Zell. Use of the Rent Roll Triangle (RRT) is not a market timing devise; it is a revenue sensitivity tool to assist you in determining areas of strength and weakness from income producing real property assets.

Use of the Rent Roll Triangle points you in the direction of particular action steps to improve financial operations, however, doing so to the exclusion of all else is folly without an over-arching plan of action that takes into account other operational aspects.

People with superior knowledge and limited experience make mistakes. So take your time with implementation of the techniques discussed herein until you understand how the concepts influence your perception of value. Here is a simple example.

A newly purchased four building asset is in dire need of new roofs, windows and paint. An inexperienced operator starts painting everything immediately thinking this is the least expensive method to increase value.

An experienced operator completes all repairs to a single building first, then moves to the next building. The experienced operator understands that having all repairs accomplished to a single building will produce higher rents for that building. Note that these "buildings" could represent four units in each building or forty units in each building. The concept remains the same.

Knowledge is power and power brings change. Prior to changing "everything" based on new knowledge slow down a little. Breathe. Contemplate. Draw up a plan of action- then implement; measure twice and cut once. This is so simple, yet so powerful.

Specialized knowledge, like that represented with Rent Roll Triangle, can cause good or evil. Said another way; do not hurt yourself with this new, sharp razor of action steps (see prior paragraph).

RRT lays out strengths and weaknesses of a rental property asset utilizing the selected variables; however, there are "always" more variables than those presented in the control group. Thus, whereas with RRT you can really shine a bright light on the variables we discuss in detail, try to avoid a myopic perspective that excludes other potential pitfalls.

Every pilot has a flight checklist called into service prior to departure of each flight. Consider RRT as part of you pre-flight, pre-acquisition checklist for rental property acquisitions.

As an owner of rental property, utilize RRT to measure your operations against potential maximum financial outputs that a rental property asset can generate. RRT will assist you in measuring present day operations against potential gains in revenue. This book will assist you in identifying and isolating operational areas to improve. The financial condition of your assets should improve incrementally from the knowledge you gain as you focus on the individual aspects of the RRT formula. You will learn the pressure points that require your attention. These will usually be the same pressure points that generate increases in cash flow, and in turn, increases in the underlying value of the assets.

# PowerHour® Books, Audio Courses & Speakers
## For Property Management Professionals & Leaders

Offers 50+ Hours of Audio Training

Featured Speakers: John Wilhoit, Jr. & Ernest F. Oriente

With a reach across 25,000,000+ multifamily units and our work in the industry since 1988, our property management clients know they can trust the PowerHour® team to offer industry books and audio courses packed with industry-specific strategies, resources and winning solutions plus industry speakers that are subject-matter experts.

www.multifamilyinsight.net/books

Copyright 2015 PowerHour®

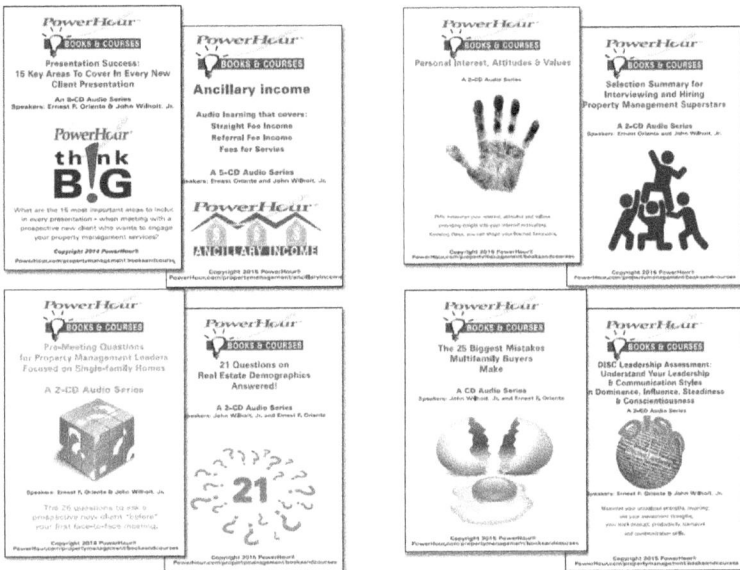

**Author:** John Wilhoit, Jr.

**Email:** jwilhoit@win-rei.om

**Website:** Multifamilyinsight.net

Ernest F. Oriente, a business coach and trainer since 1995, and a property management industry professional since 1988—and John Wilhoit, Managing Member of WIN LLC, 20+ year multifamily owner and asset manager of apartments, condominiums and townhomes, are the co–founders of PowerHour Leadership Academy Power.

Join our weekly PowerHour Leadership Academy
www.powerhourleadershipacademy.com/pm ] for leaders who want to increase their fees, expand their new business development while controlling expenses that will maximize their NOI plus increase the net worth of their company...with a focus on GRACE [Grow Revenue & Control Expenses].

- Our working together is focused on the areas below and is available for only one property management company per city:

- Grow Your Revenue...showing you 15 ways to gain more revenue, increase your new client relationships and grow your market share/impact

- Direct Competitors...working together on a 13–part presentation focused on how to out–sell and out–market those you are competing most with

- Your Team...focusing on interviewing skills, hiring best–practices, compensation plans, and the steps for training and retaining the very best

- Control Expenses...with discussions related to bids/RFPs, vendor selection and compliance and best–practices from an expert vendor/supplier perspective

# 365 CONNECT

**About 365 Connect, LLC**: Founded in 2003, award-winning *365 Connect* is the industry leader in designing and delivering an array of online platforms that work in unison with each other to market, lease and retain residents in multifamily communities. The *365 Connect Platform* interfaces with social media, management software, marketing platforms and a host of other third-party applications. It prides itself in being one of the most integration-friendly platforms in the industry and has proven to be so effective, that it has also gained acceptance with government programs in affordable housing. *365 Connect* designs technology to enhance not only the user experience for property managers, but also prospects and residents that utilize its platforms to locate, lease and live in multifamily communities nationwide.

Explore: www.365connect.com

**About MultifamilyBiz.com**: *MultifamilyBiz.com* is the Next Generation Internet Platform for the Multifamily Industry and is the place to be for everything touching multifamily housing. *MultifamilyBiz.com* covers the entire spectrum of multifamily housing, including market-rate, affordable, student and senior housing, in both the rental and for sale markets. From the latest industry news, member posted press releases, to its robust vendor directories, *MultifamilyBiz.com* is dedicated to providing a suite of focused, leading-edge, online tools and resources designed to maximize and accelerate commercial activities in the multifamily marketplace. For more information regarding *MultifamilyBiz.com* and its services visit: *www.MultifamilyBiz.com*

www.ingramcontent.com/pod-product-compliance
Lightning Source LLC
Chambersburg PA
CBHW020203200326
41521CB00005BA/236